THE BOOK OF CUSTOMER SERVICE

A No-Nonsense Guide to Earning
Trust and Keeping Customers
Coming Back

By Daniel Brewer

Jacket art: Daniel Brewer

Acknowledgment & Fair Use Notice
This book includes personal interpretations and commentary on well-known customer service concepts, including themes inspired by Bob Farrell's *Give 'Em the Pickle* and the workplace principles popularized in *Fish!*. These references are included under the Fair Use doctrine (17 U.S.C. §107) for educational and transformative purposes. All original copyrights remain with their respective owners. This book is not affiliated with, endorsed by, or licensed by any of the original publishers or authors.

Material furnished by Carl Moyer is used with his written permission.

ISBN Hard Bound: 979-8-9991679-2-7

ISBN Paperback: 979-8-9991679-0-3

ISBN Electronic Book: 979-8-9991679-1-0

http://www.custservguru.com

TO EVERY CUSTOMER
I'VE EVER SERVED

AND THOSE I HAVEN'T

...YET

TO MARY AND IAN

—

WE'VE SEEN WHAT GREAT
SERVICE LOOKS LIKE — AND
WHAT HAPPENS WHEN IT
DISAPPEARS COMPLETELY

TABLE OF CONTENTS

EPILOGUE

ACKNOWLEDGEMENTS

ABOUT THE AUTHOR

TESTIMONIALS

QUICK REFERENCE GUIDE

PROLOGUE

"A customer is the most important visitor on our premises; he is not dependent on us. We are dependent on him."

- **Mahatma Gandhi**

MY EARLY JOURNEY IN CUSTOMER SERVICE

My journey in customer service began when I was just 14 years old, working at my mother's pet shop inside a supermarket. The store had a massive tank of pool fish at the entrance to draw people in, while everything else was carefully arranged to capture their interest.

My mother and her team instilled in me the importance of presentation and customer experience. Every day, we made sure that:

- Stock items were faced forward for easy visibility.
- Price stamps were clear and readable.
- Messes and spills were cleaned up immediately.
- The glass on the large pool fish tank was spotless — several times a day.

The customer's impression was always the priority. Add a smile, a kind word, and knowledgeable service, and you could win customers for life, which we did.

About the same time, I worked Saturday mornings at a local small, family-owned store. For two hours each Saturday, my task was simple: count and separate bottles and cans for recycling. If I finished early, I'd get the chance to learn the art of bagging groceries. It wasn't just about stuffing items into a bag. It was about doing it right. Keeping like items together, never placing soap and meat in the same bag, and always asking if the customer needed help carrying groceries to their car. (Who would have known how handy that skill would be in this current era of self-checkout and bagging your own groceries?)

From there, I took a paper route, delivering newspapers every evening after school on my bicycle. No matter what the weather, my customers expected their paper on the porch before dinner.

I quickly learned an important lesson: Consistency matters. If I did my job well and on time, I might be rewarded with a nice tip when I made my monthly collection rounds.

At 16, I got my first "real job" at a popular local pizza parlor. It was large, always busy, and the food was excellent. The people I met there have remained lifelong friends, and many of the lessons I learned about customer service are highlighted in this book. (I still advocate the importance that a high school job has on so many levels) After college, I returned to the newspaper business, did some part-time teaching, and then transitioned into technology, spending 25 years in the world of technical support. I also worked as a high school basketball official for 30 seasons. This was an experience that, in its own way, reinforced the importance of rapport, communication, and handling people under pressure.

After becoming a full-time father to a special needs son, I experienced the corporate layoffs that hit my company in 2013. I went back into education for a few years as a teacher's aide and even spent three seasons as an usher for the Portland Timbers and Thorns Football

Clubs (soccer). A few years later, I started my own business as a Mobile Notary Public, a career I still pursue today as a solo entrepreneur. (You will hear more about all of this later.)

I share this background for two reasons. Since I was very young, I have worked, at some level, to create positive customer experiences. I didn't realize it then, but that's what I was doing. In every role I've held, my success has stemmed from one key mindset. I was always looking ahead to the result as seen by the person who matters most, the customer. Is the fish tank clean? Is the pizza good? Are the tables clean? Did their computer get fixed with minimal hassle? Did I have empathy for the family that needs their documents signed at the hospital? Did I allow the basketball coach to vent enough to keep my relationship strong with the players while maintaining control of the game? Do I know the rules well enough? It was always about making it easiest for the customers.

This book was born out of an assignment I was handed while working as a corporate product trainer for a large, outsourced contact center. Two of my managers noticed a stark contrast in how our many different clients approached customer service training. Some had exceptional programs in place, while others barely touched the topic (if at all). Yet we were always graded on customer satisfaction and loyalty, often with financial incentives or penalties attached.

I was tasked with designing a four-hour customer service training course that every agent would take before ever setting foot on the contact center floor, regardless of their line of business. I spent an entire summer attending customer service seminars and poring through the curriculum and writings. Some of it was fantastic, some dreadful, and some nonexistent. What became crystal clear was that companies that prioritized customer experience saw a dramatic improvement in their satisfaction scores. Scores stayed high, and customer loyalty stayed high. Once this program was implemented, we unsurprisingly saw a sharp rise in customer satisfaction across the board. From what I know, this program remains in place with that company today.

Years later, after leaving the industry, I began to see how poor customer service was becoming the norm and how it was directly affecting both customer morale and business success. Then, when the COVID-19 pandemic hit in 2020, things got even worse. Not only was business impacted, but *caring* was impacted. Around that time, I was launching my Notary Public business, and was attending a training Zoom call when someone asked one of the Mentors, *"What's the secret to gaining business and making it thrive?"*

A light bulb went off.

I already knew the secret. And I realized — why keep it to myself?

With some nudging from friends, I decided this book needed to be written. None of the ideas here are new. None are revolutionary. None are *finished*, because customers and customer service are always evolving. If only one or two insights from this book help you create a better experience for your customers, then I've done my job.

Because when you put the customer first, success will follow. Every time.

Daniel Brewer - February 2025

INTRODUCTION

"There is only one boss. The customer. And he can fire everybody in the company, from the chairman on down, simply by spending his money somewhere else."

- **Sam Walton**

HOW CAN I HELP?

Business today is challenging. The economy is recovering, and competition in your field is as strong as ever. It becomes important to hold on to any asset you can to gain an advantage in your place in the market. As such, you can take nothing for granted.

Your customers are your biggest asset. Without them, you have no business. If you lose them, your competitor can easily pick them up. If you are fortunate enough to have loyal customers, they will become your biggest advocates. There is nothing more valuable than that.

You cannot assume your customers will always be there for you. They could even leave you for reasons beyond your control. That is why, whenever a customer walks through the door, it is essential to take every measure to make them loyal, satisfied advocates for you and your business. It is foolish to allow a customer to leave and move on to a competitor due to poor customer service.

Customer service today is as bad as it has ever been — if not worse. Costs are skyrocketing, yet service quality continues to decline. Too often, customer concerns are met with apathy rather than urgency, and the idea that businesses thrive because of their customers has been replaced with indifference. We're expected to do more for ourselves — placing our own orders, checking ourselves out — while being nudged for gratuities at every turn. Wrong orders, cold food, and lackluster experiences have become the norm. Rather than demanding better, we tend to shrug and move on. Actually getting the opportunity to *talk* to a telephone representative has become next to impossible, largely because of a company's insistence that their self-help options are equally effective. (Here is a newsflash... They are not!) Unfortunately, this cycle keeps spiraling downward, with each new wave of workers inheriting a system that expects less and delivers even less in return. The pandemic only amplified this, leaving both customers and employees on edge, with patience wearing thin and quality standards slipping. It doesn't have to be this way. *You* have the power to change the narrative, to bring back the pride, energy, and excitement of great customer service. It's time to reset expectations and take pride in serving people once again.

As you read this book, try to connect your service or product to the consumer's expectations. You should be able to see opportunities to improve the level of customer service you and/or your team offer. You will gain insights from the **"Ten Commandments of Customer Service"** that will show immediate improvement in your customers' experience and your bottom line. The **"Three Steps to a Successful Interaction"** should offer a framework for making every interaction personal to the customer. (Or for that matter, anyone else you might need to talk to).

Nothing in this book is rocket science. You have heard most, if not all, of these ideas before. Also, much of what we will discuss is plain, simple, common sense. Sometimes, when you see common sense written on a page, it becomes an "Aha!" moment.

Why is this important? We live in a consumer society. Every day, more money is spent, and everyone in every industry competes for that money. Competition is fierce. Considerable factors influence how a consumer chooses one product or company over another. Convenience, speed, product quality, cost, reputation, and, yes, customer service will all play a role in how they make that decision.

These stories are as varied as the people and experiences that they have. You will read a number of these stories as this book progresses. The stories of failure are as important as the stories of success, and each can also become a story of inspiration. I want you to see an example that resonates and say, "Yep! I want to do that. This is easy." Customer Service should celebrate the positive and learn from the negative. I have no doubts that by being a small but significant part of your customers' journey, you and your business or company can get where you want to be and beyond.

WHY THIS MATTERS TO ME

I believe the reason I've found moderate success in my notary business isn't because I have the flashiest website or the biggest marketing budget. It's because I'm nice. I try to be compassionate. I treat people with respect, whether I'm sitting at a kitchen table at 8:30 p.m. helping someone sign a power of attorney, or meeting them in a parking lot to notarize a single document. I know my job. And what I don't know, I know where to look and who to ask.

I try to be as attentive as I can to the person in front of me and the details of the job. I don't multitask when I'm with a client. I don't cut corners. I don't just check boxes and move on. It's not about speed. It's about presence. And in a world where everything feels automated, cold, or transactional, that alone can set you apart.

I never ask for reviews. But they come in anyway. Why? Because when people feel heard, respected, and cared for—even in a brief professional interaction—they remember it. They talk about it. They tell their neighbors and friends. I don't need to say I'm good at what I do. My customers do it for me.

That's the thread running through this entire book. Whether you're a notary, a realtor, a barista, a small business owner, or someone working on commission, the same principles apply. Know your craft. Care about people. Stay curious. Strive to be better. Treat every customer like they matter—because they do.

You don't need a script. You don't need corporate slogans. You just need a commitment to be a decent human being who shows up with care, competence, and consistency. And if that's your starting point, you're already ahead of the game.

SOLOPRENEURS AND SMALL BUSINESS OWNERS

When I talk about customer service, I'm not just referring to employees at big companies with HR manuals and call center scripts. I'm talking about people who do everything. They're the front-line agent, the support team, and the management, all in one. In the next chapter, you'll meet Joe, Mary, Frank, and Andrea. Some of us have to be everyone.

If you're a solopreneur, a commission-based rep, or someone building a small business from the ground up, this book is especially for you. You don't just answer the phone—you are the phone system. You don't have a complaints department—you take the complaint and solve it yourself. Your reputation isn't just part of your job. It is the job.

My cousin and his wife run a small café and coffee shop. He takes orders, bakes the goods, clears the tables, and works the register. His wife helps when she can, and together they've built something special. It's not because of their budget. It's because of their care and attention. If they didn't prioritize service, they wouldn't have repeat business. They wouldn't have survived, let alone expanded to a second location.

That's what separates them from the other coffee shop just a mile away.

If that sounds familiar, then this book is for you. Because in your world, good service isn't a bonus. It's survival.

CHAPTER ONE

THE BOOK OF JOE

"If you don't appreciate your customers, someone else will."

- **Jason Langella**

WHO IS MY CUSTOMER?

When we look at who our customers are, it may seem obvious. If they come into your store, pay for a service, or are on the phone to do business, they are customers. Without your customer, you have no business. They are, in fact, your boss. What do you call a business without customers? A failed business.

In truth, everyone can be considered someone's customer in some way. Most businesses also have "internal customers." These may be peers, supervisors, or collaborators in another department. Throughout this book, I will refer to the people we serve as "*customers*," but depending on your industry, company, or even where you are in the country, they may go by a different name. In hospitality, they are often called *guests*; in healthcare, they might be *patients* or *residents*. Restaurants serve *diners*, while entertainment venues cater to *patrons* or *fans*. Subscription-based businesses have *subscribers*, and online platforms may refer to them as *users* or *members*. In education, they are *students*, while nonprofits serve *donors* or *clients*. No matter the title, the concept remains the same — they are the reason we exist, and our job is to serve them well.

I call them "The Boss" because, at the end of the day, they are the ones who determine our success. If we don't keep them happy and coming back, we won't need this book, because our business would fail. By keeping them loyal, the possibilities are boundless.

I know something about you from the outset. You are a customer service expert! I can consider this because I know you are, in fact… a customer. You have an essential role in this thought from both perspectives (as both a "customer" and a "customer service expert"). For the moment, let's think about your interactions as a customer. What do you expect?

- You want your expectations to be met. If you are buying coffee, you want your order to be correct. If you are expecting a delivery or at-home service, you want it at the time and in the manner it was promised.
- You want attentiveness. You expect that whoever is helping you will do their best for you and become your advocate.
- You want respect. Respect has become a problematic word and is under scrutiny these days. Respect is earned by actions and should be valued in kind.
- As consumers, you understand that things can and will go wrong. How the company or service recovers from mistakes can sometimes mean more to a customer than the original service. Customers want it made right, and we want to assure satisfaction. Mostly, we want them to tell others and say, "I'll be back."

As we continue to discuss the many different relationships in customer service, I want to offer you a frame of reference. You may not always realize who your real customer is!

Let me introduce you to some people:

THE END-USER (JOE)

In the end, Joe is everyone's guy. He is the one we are working to please. In simple terms, he is the one who provides the money. Maybe Joe isn't directly signing your paycheck (that comes from your company, employer, or client), but ultimately, we all know where the money originates — it's in Joe's pocket.

Joe goes by many names: *End-user, Consumer, Customer, Guest, or Client.* While Burger-Freeze may be the company issuing my paycheck, their revenue — and my paycheck — ultimately comes from Joe. Without him, there is no business. Joe is at the end of the money chain, making him the most important person in the process.

WHO IS JOE?

- A diner walking into a restaurant
- A customer stepping into a retail store
- A purchaser browsing a car lot
- A caller reaching out to a contact center for support, billing, sales, or other assistance
- An end-user navigating a website to access products or services
- A traveler booking a flight or checking into a hotel
- A patient scheduling an appointment at a clinic or hospital
- A student enrolling in an online course or university program
- A gamer purchasing in-game content or a new console
- An End-user on a free website or search engine viewing the ads placed before them
- A homeowner calling for repairs or renovations
- A subscriber renewing a magazine, streaming service, or software license

Joe is everywhere, and no matter the industry, our success depends on keeping him happy.

MY FRIENDS AT WORK (MARY)

Mary is the first person at my business to whom Joe talks. She isn't just serving customers — she is a customer herself. For Joe to receive the product or service he needs, many people must perform well for Mary. In many cases, she is treated more like a co-worker than a customer, but she should be treated as both.

Take the Burger-Freeze example: the cooks in the back may not realize it, but they have two customers, Mary *and* Joe. Mary relies on the kitchen staff, inventory team, and management to do their jobs so she can do hers. Without her, Joe doesn't get served properly.

However, Mary is being removed from the chain more and more, replaced by technology. When ordering from Amazon, for example, we don't interact with a human. The only person we might see is the delivery driver — unless something goes wrong, which happens only a fraction of the time.

In this Amazon scenario, Mary is a computer interface. That website must be as customer-friendly and helpful as Mary would be if she were standing right in front of Joe. We've all been there, excited to buy something, only to get frustrated with a clunky website and give up, thinking, "Forget it, I'll just drive to Walmart."

Mary is always present in some form. Whether she's a person or a digital system, she plays a critical role in keeping Joe satisfied. Without her, the customer experience breaks down.

WHO IS MARY?

Mary could be:

- A bank teller assisting with transactions and account inquiries
- An "Orange Apron" associate at Home Depot helping customers find what they need
- A server or front-of-house host/hostess at a restaurant greeting and seating guests

- A Customer Service Associate (CSA) in a contact center handling support, billing, or sales
- A car salesperson (or any salesperson) guiding customers through a purchase
- A hotel receptionist checking in guests and answering questions
- A retail cashier processing purchases and assisting with returns
- A grocery store clerk helping customers locate items or assisting at checkout
- Tech support representative troubleshooting product issues
- A pharmacist or pharmacy technician ensuring customers get the right medication
- A flight attendant assisting passengers during their journey
- A receptionist at a doctor's office scheduling appointments and welcoming patients
- A customer service rep on a live chat helping with online orders
- A help desk associate in an electronics store explaining product features

Mary is the bridge between Joe and the business. Whether in person, over the phone, or through a digital interface, she ensures Joe gets what he needs.

"VIRTUAL MARY"

More and more, businesses are replacing human interaction with technology, creating what I will call *Virtual Mary*. She is the self-service alternative to a live employee, guiding customers through their transactions without direct human assistance. Whether it's a self-checkout kiosk at the grocery store, an order screen at Taco Bell, or an automated chat system on a website, Virtual Mary is designed to provide the same service as a real person, just faster and often with fewer errors.

Some businesses, like Amazon, rely almost entirely on Virtual Mary. From product searches to order placement, tracking, and returns, nearly every customer interaction is handled through an automated system. The only time a human gets involved is when something goes wrong, which happens only a small percentage of the time. While Virtual Mary improves efficiency and lowers costs for businesses, she can also be frustrating for customers when systems are confusing or lack the personal touch of a real employee.

WHERE DO WE SEE "VIRTUAL MARY?"

- Self-checkout kiosks in grocery stores, big-box retailers, and pharmacies
- Ordering kiosks at fast food restaurants like Taco Bell and McDonald's
- ATM machines replacing bank tellers for withdrawals and deposits
- Mobile ordering apps for restaurants, coffee shops, and stores
- Automated chatbots handling customer service inquiries online
- Virtual assistants like Siri, Alexa, and Google Assistant answering questions
- Ride-sharing apps (Uber, Lyft) where the entire process is digital–Until the driver shows up, then Virtual Mary becomes *Actual* Mary
- Airline websites and kiosks for check-in and boarding pass printing
- Streaming service recommendations and customer support (Netflix, Spotify, etc.)
- Contactless hotel check-ins using mobile apps instead of front desk staff

Virtual Mary is becoming more common as companies look for ways to cut costs and streamline customer experiences. While she provides speed and convenience, she also lacks the flexibility and warmth of human interaction. For businesses, the challenge is ensuring Virtual Mary enhances the customer experience rather than frustrating users.

A well-designed Virtual Mary can keep Joe happy, but a poorly implemented one might send him looking for a company where a real person is still available to help.

While Virtual Mary handles most interactions smoothly, there will always be moments when a human is needed. Escalations, unusual requests, or system errors may require intervention from a real person. Let's not forget — someone must design, program, and maintain Virtual Mary to keep her running efficiently.

BEHIND THE SCENES (FRANK OR FRAN)

In many companies, the people working *behind the scenes* far outnumber those on the front lines. In businesses that operate mostly or entirely online, *everyone* is technically behind the scenes. Just because these employees don't interact directly with Joe doesn't mean they aren't critical to his experience.

At Burger-Freeze, for example, Frank might be the line cook, the product stocker, the maintenance worker, or the janitor. He may never speak to Joe, but his work directly affects Joe's satisfaction. A well-prepared meal, stocked supplies, clean floors, and working equipment all contribute to the seamless experience that Joe expects. A messy dining area, a broken soda machine, or a missing ingredient in an order might be enough to make Joe take his money elsewhere.

Frank's role extends far beyond restaurants. In almost every industry, there are countless professionals ensuring that Mary has the tools she needs to serve Joe. Programmers keep systems running, analysts track customer behavior, and trainers prepare employees for success. Without Frank, Mary can't do her job, and if Mary can't do her job, Joe walks away unhappy.

WHO IS FRANK?

- A line cook preparing meals for restaurant guests
- A product stocker ensuring shelves are full and inventory is available

- A maintenance worker keeping equipment running smoothly
- A janitor maintaining a clean and inviting environment
- A programmer or IT specialist developing and maintaining software for Virtual Mary
- A data analyst studying trends to improve customer experience
- A project manager coordinating teams to ensure efficiency and quality
- A trainer educating employees on processes, customer service, and best practices
- An HR professional hiring and supporting the team that serves Joe
- A warehouse worker packing and shipping online orders
- A graphic designer creating user-friendly websites and marketing materials
- A financial analyst ensuring budgets and resources are allocated effectively
- A security officer protecting customers, employees, and business assets
- A groundskeeper or landscaper keeping the campus or parking area looking inviting to employees and clients.

Frank may not always be visible, but his impact is undeniable. Whether flipping burgers, coding websites, or analyzing customer data, he plays a vital role in making sure Mary has everything she needs to serve Joe. Without Frank, the entire system falls apart.

THE MANAGEMENT TEAM (ANDREW OR ANDREA)

It's easy to assume that managers don't have customers because they don't interact directly with Joe every day. That assumption couldn't be further from the truth. Andrew or Andrea, whether they are a team manager, assistant manager, shift supervisor, or CEO, has a wide range of customers to serve. In fact, their role is about ensuring that the people who interact with Joe — Mary, Frank, and others — have what they need to perform at their best.

Managers like Andrew are responsible for making sure that Frank has the tools, support, and resources to help Mary do her job well. They must ensure that Mary has the training, guidance, and environment she needs to serve Joe. Of course, Andrew must make sure that Joe leaves satisfied, with his needs met and expectations exceeded.

But Andrew does not just serve those directly under him. Managers are also responsible for keeping their superiors happy, whether that is answering to higher-level managers, the company's CEO, or shareholders. Even the CEO has their own customers: investors, board members, and owners who they need to keep satisfied to maintain their job. Management's role is to keep the entire chain running smoothly, ensuring that everyone, whether it is Mary, Joe, or the company's shareholders, is taken care of.

WHO IS ANDREW (OR ANDREA)?

Andrea could be:

- A team manager overseeing day-to-day operations and supporting direct reports
- An assistant manager ensuring systems run smoothly and stepping in for shifts as needed
- A shift supervisor coordinating the work and ensuring quality during each shift
- A department manager responsible for overseeing an entire department or service area
- A project manager ensuring deadlines are met, teams are aligned, and resources are available
- A store or branch manager ensuring customers are served well and that the store runs efficiently
- A regional manager overseeing multiple locations and ensuring consistency in service and operations

- An executive manager making strategic decisions that guide company direction
- A CEO balancing the needs of employees, customers, investors, and board members
- A founder or owner ensuring the company's values and goals align with stakeholder interests

Andrew (or Andrea) isn't just a manager — he or she is the linchpin that keeps the operation running smoothly. Whether managing a single team or a whole company, their job is to ensure that Frank, Mary, and Joe all have what they need to succeed. In a way, every level of management serves multiple customers: the employees below them, the company above them, and, of course, the end customers like Joe and Mary. Management is the glue that holds everything together, ensuring the entire system functions harmoniously.

CUSTOMER SERVICE: THE FINAL FRONTIER

When I look at a company's customer infrastructure, I cannot help but think of one of my favorite TV shows of the 1960s, *Star Trek*. Stay with me for a moment. If you pay attention to the colors of the uniforms, you will see an uncanny resemblance to the roles within any business. Understanding these roles through a Starfleet lens might just give you a fresh perspective on customer service, Jim!

Gold Shirts – Operations (Command & Direct Service)

In Star Trek, gold shirts were worn by the captains and officers responsible for leading the mission. In business, this represents Andrea and Mary, those in direct contact with Joe (the star of our episode). Managers, supervisors, and front-line employees wear metaphorical gold shirts because they make real-time decisions that directly affect the customer experience.

Blue Shirts – Support (Science, Strategy & Back-Office Operations)

In Star Trek, blue shirts were worn by scientists, doctors, and analysts, the thinkers behind the mission. In business, these are your support teams: HR, training, quality assurance, finance, data analysts, and even warehouse or corporate office employees.

Frank might wear a blue shirt if he works in a cubicle, warehouse, or corporate office, handling payroll, inventory, reporting, or logistics. He may never interact with Joe, but he plays a critical role in ensuring everything behind the scenes runs smoothly so that Mary and Andrea can focus on Joe.

Red Shirts – Infrastructure (Engineering, IT & Maintenance)

Yes, in pop culture, red shirts have a reputation for not surviving the episode. They were engineers, tech specialists, and mechanics. They kept the ship running. In business, there are IT professionals, developers, custodians, facilities managers, and equipment technicians. People who build, fix, and maintain everything that allows Mary and Andrea to serve Joe. Without Red Shirts, systems crash, stores stay messy, and technology breaks, making it impossible for Mary to do her job.

Think of a school setting: The students are the customers. The janitors, cafeteria workers, and IT specialists may not teach lessons, but their role is just as crucial in shaping the students' experience.

Whether you are wearing gold, blue, or red, your job impacts whether Joe remains a loyal customer or beams out to a competitor. No role is insignificant. A ship (or business) doesn't succeed unless every crew member is working together toward the mission: keeping Joe happy.

THE TEN-BY-TEN RULE

This is as good a time as any to mention the 10 x 10 rule (ten-by-ten). This refers to two essential principles. It is suggested that each person who has a good experience with you might tell someone else, maybe even ten people. However, each person who has a poor experience will *also* tell everyone, or theoretically, ten other people. For each customer you lose because of poor Customer Service, you must regain *ten* new loyal customers to compensate for it. People talk to each other. That can be great for good experiences, but miserable for bad. One thing is for sure, crappy customer service is a lousy reason to lose a loyal customer. You want the "word of mouth" that will result from your interaction to be in your favor.

In the past, this principle was driven by personal recommendations and conversations, but with the rise of social media, the impact is magnified exponentially. A single bad review, negative post, or viral complaint can spread to thousands — if not millions — of people in an instant. (Yep, *Nextdoor* is a real thing!) On the flip side, exceptional customer service can generate the same level of exposure in a positive way, turning satisfied customers into loyal advocates who promote your business for free. The takeaway? Delivering outstanding customer experiences isn't just about retention; it's about leveraging the power of social media to drive your business into the stratosphere.

Sometimes, things just go sideways for no good reason. It could be because of a mistake you or one of your peers made, for reasons outside of your control, or for no reason at all. How you *recover* from an unpleasant experience with your customer can even offer a better impression than if things went smoothly. Prices change, expectations are set high, you are out of stock, and the customer comes into your establishment thinking of one thing when, in fact, it is another. (We have all been to the DMV, right?) How you react and how you can "make it right" will go far in saving a customer who could leave angry.

I once had a notary customer who called me and was incensed with the fees I charged, such as a travel fee. (Which is standard practice for the industry.) He started to get angry and said he might as well just go to the UPS store. They are free or very cheap. I surprised him and simply told him that it might be a good option for him. I looked up UPS stores local to him and their hours, and offered my services in case the UPS store could not help him. He thanked me and hung up. He was not angry but grateful that I understood. I did not get the customer, but I maintained the relationship in case he needed my services at another time. If he were to review that interaction, I have no doubt he would do so favorably.

INDUSTRY VS. INDUSTRY: THE CUSTOMER SERVICE BATTLEGROUND

Customer service isn't just a competitive advantage for individual companies; it shapes entire industries. When one sector or company lets its guard down, others seize the opportunity to win over customers. Below are four industries where customer service has created significant shifts in market share.

BANKING: THE CREDIT UNION EDGE

Large national banks often struggle with customer satisfaction in the banking world, weighed down by bureaucracy, fees, and impersonal service. Many think they are still recovering from the 2008 banking crisis, and they might well be. While some regional and community banks maintain strong reputations, those that expand aggressively through mergers and acquisitions often lose their personal touch. Meanwhile, credit unions, being nonprofit and member-focused, consistently outrank big banks in customer satisfaction. They prioritize relationships over revenue, proving that customer-first models drive loyalty in financial services.

FAST FOOD: GROWTH VS. CUSTOMER EXPERIENCE

Fast food chains often face a tug-of-war between expansion and maintaining service quality. In-N-Out Burger built a cult following with its simple menu, fresh ingredients, and legendary customer service. Still, as it expands beyond its West Coast roots, and it is doing so very slowly and carefully, there's concern about whether it can scale while keeping its high standards. Starbucks faced a similar issue. After dominating the coffee market, they diluted their brand by expanding into entertainment, food, and even alcohol sales. Competitors like Dutch Bros, which kept customer experience as its #1 priority, seized market share. Starbucks has since refocused on its core coffee business, slowly regaining customer trust, but its stumble shows how easy it is to lose ground. (Or in this case…grounds!)

E-COMMERCE: AMAZON'S DOMINANCE AND CHALLENGERS

Amazon has ruled e-commerce for over two decades, especially since COVID-19 solidified its dominance. It was a true retail disruptor. Its relentless focus on convenience, fast shipping, and hassle-free returns has made it nearly unbreakable. However, new challengers like Temu and Wayfair are trying to carve out niches, using aggressive pricing and marketing to lure customers. Amazon, unlike past tech giants that lost focus, continues to double down on its customer-first model, keeping it at the top. The lesson? Disruptors can make inroads, but the market leader only loses when they shift priorities away from customers.

SEARCH ENGINES: THE RISE AND FALL OF YAHOO!

Yahoo! once dominated the internet. For its first decade, it was the undisputed king of search, news, and email. However, after going public, it shifted focus to maximizing ad revenue and appeasing shareholders rather than improving its core user experience. This shift opened the door for Google, which kept its ads in the background and prioritized a clean, fast, user-friendly experience. Even though some of Google's products are not the most innovative, it remains the dominant search engine because it never forgot that users come first. Meanwhile, Yahoo! became cluttered, lost its identity, and faded into irrelevance.

IT'S GETTING AWAY FROM US

During research for this book, an interesting perspective on the difficulty in getting person-to-person service in retail and food service emerged.

A question was posed:

"At McDonald's, customers were choosing to wait in line for a cashier rather than using the available kiosks. Why might that be?"

A common response, shared by many, reflected a growing frustration with self-service technology.

One individual expressed a firm stance against self-checkouts, refusing to use them even when faced with long lines or encouragement from staff. The reasoning behind this was simple. While businesses often cite labor costs as their biggest expense, the expectation would be that reduced staff levels should lead to lower prices. However, prices continue to rise despite these cuts.

A personal example was shared regarding a local Home Depot. Over time, the store's service quality declined, stock levels dropped, and knowledgeable staff became harder to find. Eventually, all traditional checkout lanes were replaced with self-service kiosks. As a result, the customer stopped shopping there, opting instead for competitors like Canadian Tire and Ace Lumberworld, where they could still receive assistance from actual employees.

The broader concern was that self-checkouts are part of a larger corporate strategy to maximize profits while offering consumers lower-quality goods and diminished service. A similar issue arises in technical support. Rather than receiving direct assistance, customers are often forced to navigate self-help knowledge bases, submit online forms, and endure long wait times before reaching a human representative.

For this individual, refusing to use self-checkouts is a personal protest against the decreasing value consumers receive for their money. While they acknowledge that their resistance may be in vain, they take comfort in knowing they are making a conscious choice to support businesses that still prioritize human service.

SERVICE WITH A SHRUG

Let's talk about a very common generic scenario. Let's say you need information or support on a product or service and would like to talk to someone on the phone about it. It could be very simple; it should never be hard.

Locating a phone number is often the first hurdle; it is often buried on the website. Companies heavily push self-help options, directing customers to FAQs, troubleshooting guides, and forums before revealing a way to speak with a person. Many businesses also force users to interact with a screener before allowing access to a live representative.

Once the phone number is found, customers are met with *IVRs (Interactive Voice Response systems)* — a frustrating series of automated menus. The system rarely provides a direct path to a human, leading to wasted time navigating prompts. Finally, the dreaded waiting time: being informed they are caller #38 in the queue.

When a live agent is finally reached, they are often empathetic but not necessarily effective. Many issues require multiple agents and transfers, meaning customers must repeat their problem and go through the same security verification multiple times. The lack of internal communication between representatives drags out the process (If you do not get hung up in the process).

Once the call concludes, customers are bombarded with requests to rate their experience. Even after providing feedback, the reminders may continue. On top of that, customers are often added to marketing lists, receiving unwanted promotions.

Occasionally, a company will follow up to ensure the issue was resolved, but this is far from guaranteed. Often, the burden falls on the customer to restart the entire process if the problem persists. This cycle leaves customers feeling exhausted, undervalued, and increasingly frustrated with the decline in real human interaction.

LINES, LINES, EVERYWHERE LINES

Since smartphones became mainstream, consumers have come to expect speed and efficiency. Online grocery shopping eliminates long store visits. Food delivery services like *DoorDash* and *Grubhub* bring meals to the doorstep. Ridesharing apps such as *Uber* and *Lyft* revolutionized the taxi industry by making transportation seamless. People will *"Catch an Uber"* now when they would never "call for a taxi."

Despite the shift toward convenience, in-store shoppers still expect efficiency. Yet they are often met with long lines and slow service. There was a time when, if checkout lines got too long, a manager would call for backup over the PA system. Now, many businesses fail to prioritize speedy service for their loyal, in-person customers.

A particularly frustrating example was an in-mall retailer that had only one exchange line open during the busy week between Christmas and New Year's. This is a time when retailers should focus on moving lines quickly so customers can continue shopping. Instead, long waits drive shoppers away — possibly for good.

A core principle of great customer service is to reduce waiting times as much as possible. Long lines lead to frustration, lost sales, and negative customer experiences. (And let's be honest — we were all thinking about the DMV as the ultimate example of slow service!) Shoppers are willing to show up in person for a human experience. Businesses should respect that by keeping the lines moving!

UPSELLING TO A FAULT

Look, I get it! Marketing is important, and a customer standing right in front of you is a golden opportunity to suggest a few extras. But there's a line between helpful and pushy, and crossing it too often just drives people away. Take Home Depot, for example. If you track down one of those "orange aproned" employees for something simple — say, an electrical switch — don't be surprised if they also mention wiring, lighting options, tools, and maybe even a whole remodeling kit. Are they trying to upsell you? A little, sure. But in many cases, they're trying to make sure you don't get home, start the project, and realize you forgot something crucial. That's useful.

Now, let's contrast that with a certain battery and bulb chain I frequent. I walk in needing one thing — please change the battery for my car key fob — and immediately, I'm on guard. I know what's coming: the loyalty program pitch, the AA battery sales reminder (because apparently, we're all chronically low on AAs), and the subtle suggestion that maybe I should browse around for a backup flashlight or two. No, thanks. Just change the battery and let me get on with my day. It's gotten to the point where, for minor battery needs, I'll avoid that store altogether just to skip the gauntlet of upselling. There's a balance to be struck. Find it, and your customers will thank you.

JUST LET ME CHECK OUT, ALREADY

With the rise of self-checkout, we've gained speed and convenience — or at least we were supposed to. But what's happened is that many stores have turned checkout into a nine-screen interrogation, thinly disguised as "enhanced customer experience." Sometimes, I just want to buy a thing and leave. Now it's:

- Can I get your loyalty club number?
- Do you have a discount code?
- Are you eligible for a veteran's discount?
- Would you like to apply for our in-store credit card and get 20% off this purchase?
- Did you find everything okay?
- How many bags did you use? (In my state, paper bags cost 10 cents each.)
- Do you want cash back?
- Are you sure?
- Is this the correct amount? (Okay, I kind of like that one, it's saved me a few times.)

But here's the thing — timing matters...

Once, my wife was checking out with my special needs son, and self-checkout quickly turned into a landmine. That area is already loaded with an abundance of sensory distractions such as candy, gadgets, and blinking lights. Having to stand still for a few minutes becomes a recipe for meltdown. All we needed was to pay and go. Fast. Instead, we got stuck in the checkout maze. In a traditional checkout lane, you might get asked one or two questions. However, with self-checkout, it feels like taking a survey just to earn the right to give them your money.

We're not here for that. Sometimes, the best customer service is just speed and simplicity. Get me in, get me out.

THE TRAP OF "HELPFUL" TECHNOLOGY

Behind the scenes, Frank and his team have one primary goal: to ensure systems work effectively for the customer. Instead, what we're seeing more and more is technology that adds friction rather than removes it. When designed poorly or with the wrong goals in mind, these systems don't help — they hijack our time, our patience, and sometimes our wallets.

THE LAUNDRY APP THAT BROKE THE SPIRIT

My recently retired brother-in-law — who sold his house to hit the national dog show circuit and see the country in his new RV, accompanied by his Staffordshire Terriers — found himself parked in a lovely Midwest town, with a bit of downtime and a pile of dirty clothes. He spotted a laundromat with room for his rig and thought, "Perfect. Quick in-and-out." He grabs his soap, his quarters, and hauls it all inside — no coin slots—just a QR code.

Crap! There's an app.

Out to the lot to get a signal. Download. Create an account — hand over all his info. Make up a password. Dig out the credit card. Enter the number, the date, that little secret code. CAPTCHA wants bicycles, then motorcycles, and then stairs. Finally, success? Nope — declined. Start over? Not a chance. He rage-quits, packs up, and drives 20 miles to the next town where the machines happily take a quarter and don't ask for his mother's maiden name.

As he fumed down the highway, it hit him: it wasn't about the app — it was about Frank. The behind-the-scenes Frank who decided that what customers want when they're hauling dirty jeans is a forced software install and a side of data harvesting. My brother-in-law, who writes code for a living, took the hint: no more making people wrestle with digital tollbooths just to do a basic task. His dog show app? Login is gone. Value first, ask later. Frank? Frank should be sentenced to spend a long weekend doing laundry with nothing but that app and a spotty cell signal, so he can see how fun he's made it for the rest of us.

THE PARKING "CONVENIENCE" THAT ISN'T

Then there was my wife's recent downtown adventure. She used to work in the city, but these days only goes in for special occasions. On one of those rare trips, she found street parking and went to pay. Gone were the old coin meters; now it's a kiosk that only takes debit cards. She paid for three hours, printed the ticket, and went about her business. The next day, her bank froze her account over a suspicious charge: "Are you sure you wanted to pay $39.95 to Parking Kitty yesterday?" The actual fee should have been $6.

Once they had her card, it was open season. She declined the charge, and eventually they corrected it — but now she's left wondering when the next mystery charge will appear, simply because she dared to park for an afternoon.

We shouldn't have to risk fraud, data harvesting, or unnecessary hassle just to do the ordinary things that keep our lives moving. But too often, the Franks of the world forget that. The systems they design create obstacles, not solutions. And all we're asking is simple: let us wash our jeans, park our cars, and grab a sandwich without handing over our wallet and our data at every turn.

CAN I SWITCH YOU TO E-STATEMENTS?"

Everyone wants to go electronic now. And sure, I get it — it's efficient, it's cheaper, and everything lives on your phone. But there's a fine line between automation and abandonment.

I used to get Toastmaster magazine in the mail every month as a member of my local chapter. It came like clockwork. I'd read it within a few days and thoroughly enjoyed it. During COVID, to save money, they went digital-only. Now it ends up buried in spam folders or lost in inbox clutter. I haven't read a single issue since.

Same with my bank. Same with my utilities. They all moved to e-statements — and now I don't even glance at them. Maybe that's okay. My payments are on autopilot. But something feels missing. A paper statement, a real magazine — they caught your eye. They gave the message weight.

I'm not saying we should go back to eight-page cable bills. However, if you're going to automate something, make sure it actually adds to the customer experience, not just saves you time or money. Because if customers stop noticing what you send them, maybe it's not worth sending anymore.

THE THREE-LEGGED STOOL OF QUALITY, SERVICE, AND SPEED

One of the most memorable scenes from the movie *The Founder* (about the early days of McDonald's) is when Ray Kroc visits the original McDonald's in San Bernardino. He orders lunch and is stunned when his food is handed to him immediately after paying. Talking to customers, he learns that travelers and young families frequently stop there, two demographics that still drive the fast-food industry today.

Customer Expectations rely on three key elements:

- **Quality** – Fresh, accurate, and well-prepared orders.
- **Service** – Friendly and efficient customer interactions.
- **Speed** – Quick turnaround times to meet customer expectations.

If *any one* of these collapses, the entire customer experience falls apart.

Imagine you're in between meetings on a packed day. You stop at your favorite fast food place along "fast food row" (every busy area has one). Six minutes later, you're back on the road, reaching into the bag, only to find your order is wrong. You're hungry, in a hurry, and it's still edible, so you eat it and move on. No big deal, right? You are thinking, "They got me this time." Maybe, maybe not.

Now it is two weeks later, and you're in the same situation. But this time, you remember, "Last time, they got my order wrong." So, instead of stopping there, you choose a different restaurant. There, in the same six minutes, you get a meal that's hot, correct, and delicious. The next time you pass by the original place? You don't even consider stopping. That once-favorite spot is now dead to you, simply because they didn't take five extra seconds to double-check the bag.

A small mistake can cost long-term loyalty. Businesses that prioritize quality, service, and speed equally will keep customers coming back. Those that don't? They'll slowly fade away.

Across industries, the companies that stay focused on customer service consistently win while those that chase expansion, revenue, or trends at the expense of their customers eventually fall. Whether it's banks, fast food, e-commerce, or search engines, the lesson is clear. Customer service isn't just about keeping people happy. It determines who leads and who falls behind.

Author's Note:

At the end of each chapter, you'll find a few actions and questions to help apply what you've read. Use them as a guide — or a challenge.

▶ **Define Your Role in Customer Service.**

Consider where you fit in the broader customer experience. Are you more like Joe, Mary, Frank, or Andrea in your daily work? Do you take a front-facing role, a behind-the-scenes support position, or somewhere in between?

▶ **Reflect on what "color shirt" you metaphorically wear.**

Gold, Blue, or Red — and how that shapes your interactions. Own your role and how it contributes to the overall service mission.

▶ **Understand Who Your Customers Are.**

Your customers may include both external clients and internal teammates. Joe might be your client, but Mary, Frank, and Andrea may depend on you just as much.

▶ **List out who relies on you day to day.**

Do not dwell on just who pays the bills, but who counts on your clarity, effort, and responsiveness.

▶ **Improve the Experience for Each Group.**

Each customer group has different expectations. The way you serve a team member might differ from how you treat a client, but both deserve great service. Choose one group you serve and identify a small way you could make their experience better, easier, or more thoughtful.

Commit to One New Action Step.

Small changes often create a big impact. Maybe it's a faster response time, a thank-you note, or offering proactive updates.

Pick one thing you're not doing now but could start doing today that would immediately elevate someone's experience.

CHAPTER TWO

THE BOOK OF LOYALTY

"Loyal customers, they don't just come back, they don't simply recommend you, they insist that their friends do business with you."

- **Chip R. Bell**

SATISFIED AND LOYAL

Satisfaction is important, but it doesn't always equal loyalty. Plenty of customers leave satisfied but never return. Loyalty is about something deeper — an emotional connection, a reason to choose you over the competition. Here are some key factors:

Price/Value:

If your prices aren't competitive, customers might leave even if they love your product.

Convenience:

Even the best businesses lose customers to more convenient options. If a competitor is closer, faster, or easier, loyalty can disappear.

Quality:

No matter how great your customer service is, if your product or service declines, customers will eventually move on.

Attention to Detail:

Small things, like having an item in stock or making online ordering seamless, can make the difference between keeping or losing a customer.

Now, let's break down four types of customer experiences using real-world examples. Look at the grid below. It illustrates how customer satisfaction and loyalty come together to drive real results. As customers ourselves, we know what great service looks like.

From your own consumer experiences, which businesses truly create both satisfied and loyal customers, and which ones seem to focus on just one while neglecting the other? In short… Where do you spend your money?

	LOYAL	NOT LOYAL
SATISFIED		
NOT SATISFIED		

SATISFIED AND LOYAL (THE GOLD STANDARD)

These are the businesses that get it right. Customers are happy, and they keep coming back. According to consumer surveys and articles, some of the top-rated companies for customer service include:

Trader Joe's:

Not the biggest selection, but customers love their personalized experience and community-driven approach.

Amazon:

Fast shipping, easy returns, and proactive customer service make them a global leader in loyalty. They started as a retail disruptor and have maintained high customer service standards for more than 20 years.

State Farm:

Their "like a good neighbor" motto reflects their strong reputation for service.

Your Favorite Local Business:

Think of a small business that makes you feel valued every time you walk in. Why do customers return? Because these businesses listen, respond, and make the experience effortless.

THE LOYAL HAIRCUT

When my son was growing up, haircuts were a battle. He has special needs and has always had trouble sitting still, especially with the noise and sensory overload of a strip mall salon. We tried the usual quick-cut places, and occasionally, we'd find someone who just *got it*. One of those was someone I will call Terry. The moment we walked in, she could tell we needed a different approach. She skipped the cape, listened patiently, gave our son a quick, no-drama buzz cut, and told us to ask for her directly next time. Eventually, she gave me her email address and said if things ever got tough, she'd even come to our house. For a few years, thanks to her, we had the haircut issue handled.

Then, like so many great service providers, she moved on to another field, and we lost touch.

Then COVID hit. Nobody was getting haircuts, and my wife — God bless her — gave it a go. But let's be honest, she's not a barber. Our son's hair got longer, and he liked it, so the buzz-cut was out. But after a year, we needed help. I remembered Terry's card and contacted her, hoping she could refer someone. To my surprise, she replied right away. She'd started renting a salon space three days a week and was focusing on men's hair. She told us to come in, and we did. Her prices were higher now, but it is worth every penny. Now, she books us both in the same slot, gets two cuts and two tips, and we leave with minimal stress. That kind of service doesn't just win a customer. It earns a loyal one for life.

	LOYAL	NOT LOYAL
SATISFIED	Lowe's Trader Joe's State Farm Amazon Your favorite local business	
NOT SATISFIED		

SATISFIED BUT NOT LOYAL (CONVENIENCE OVER COMMITMENT)

These are businesses that get the job done, but customers don't necessarily feel a strong connection. Examples:

7-Eleven:

You might grab a snack there, but would you drive across town just to visit a specific location? Probably not. (However, because of some of the personal touches provided by the crew, you might find more loyalty there.)

Subway:

The sandwich is fine, but you'd eat at any sandwich shop that's nearby.

Gas Stations (Union 76, Shell, etc.):

People usually just go to the closest or cheapest one.

Fast Food Chains (McDonald's, Burger King, etc.):

They're everywhere, and you'll eat at whichever one is convenient at the moment. These businesses rely on volume, location, and price, not necessarily customer loyalty.

	LOYAL	NOT LOYAL
SATISFIED	Lowe's Trader Joe's State Farm Amazon Your favorite local business	7-11 Subway Union 76 McDonald's
NOT SATISFIED		

Loyal, but not satisfied? Huh!? This one sounds even stranger than the last one, doesn't it? Ever had a company you *wish* you could leave but can't? These businesses don't prioritize customer happiness, but they keep customers because there aren't many alternatives.

Utility Companies (Electric, Water, Trash):

No competition means no urgency to provide great service. (Also, in some places, contracts are locally negotiated, so you may have no choice at all.) Also, prices can rise on a whim without much resistance.

DMV/Government Agencies:

Long wait times, lack of urgency, and poor service, but you have no choice.

Telecom Companies (Internet & Cable Providers):

You may hate dealing with them, but switching is a hassle. You may have a favorite here, but that is rare. Trust me! These businesses survive not on loyalty, but necessity — a dangerous place to be in an evolving market.

	LOYAL	NOT LOYAL
SATISFIED	Lowe's Trader Joe's State Farm Amazon Your favorite local business	7-11 Subway Union 76 McDonald's
NOT SATISFIED	DMV Electric Company Trash Services Telecom companies	

This list will infuriate some and instill passion in others. Think of places you have been that have lost you as a customer forever.

This is the *danger zone*. These are companies with bad service, no loyalty, and no compelling reason for customers to return. Every year, surveys list the worst customer service offenders. Below are some industries that have repeat offenders:

Certain Internet & Cable Companies:

High prices, bad customer support, and unexpected fees drive customers away.

Banks & Credit Card Companies:

Some have a reputation for poor service, hidden charges, and long phone wait times.

Retail Chains with Poor Service:

Some big-box stores cut back on employees, leaving customers struggling to find help.

Event Ticket Brokerage companies:

Hidden fees, bad websites, and setting improper expectations. (Just tell me how much the ticket costs, okay?) A $75 seat just cost me $135, and I have no idea why.

Once a company ends up on a customer's personal "never again" list, it's nearly impossible to win them back.

EIGHTY-FIVE BUCKS AND STILL HUNGRY

One recent weekend, we were busy and knew we'd be hitting the fast-food circuit for a couple of days. First stop: a sandwich shop known for its speed. We ordered three full meals — sandwiches, chips, and drinks — for around $50. Pricey, but okay. What did we get? Some limp cold cuts on a dry roll with a sad slice of tomato. No cheese, no mayo, nothing resembling what we expected, or what a sandwich even looks like. Now, I get that speed is their thing — but maybe spend an extra ten seconds making the food worth eating? With so many sandwich shops in our area, we won't be going back. We'll find someone who can be fast *and* get it right.

The next day, we tried a drive-thru Chinese place. You know the drill — the first question is always, "Chow Mein or fried rice?" I said fried rice. I *always* say fried rice. But when we opened the bag at the park, surprise: Chow Mein. Another $35 wasted. That's $85 in two days, and not one correct or decent meal. Loyal? Not even close. Satisfied? Not a chance. The bar isn't that high — get the order right, make the food edible, and treat the customer like they matter. Give yourself fifteen more seconds. It makes all the difference.

	LOYAL	NOT LOYAL
SATISFIED	Lowe's Trader Joe's State Farm Amazon Your favorite local business	7-11 Subway Union 76 McDonald's
NOT SATISFIED	DMV Electric Company Trash Services Telecom companies	AOL Comcast Sprint Capital One Time Warner "Ticket King"

Look at the grid below and think about your own experiences. Where do you like to spend your money? Which businesses have earned your loyalty? Which ones have lost you forever? Are there places you still go, not because you want to, but because you have no other choice?

Now, take a moment and fill out the grid based on your own experiences. As you do ask the favorite question of every 4-year-old: **Why?**

- ▶ Why do you love this business?
- ▶ What do they do differently that keeps you coming back?
- ▶ What businesses have lost you as a customer?
- ▶ Why will you never go there again?
- ▶ What was the breaking point?
- ▶ What's the difference between satisfaction and loyalty?
- ▶ What does it take for a company to move from "good enough" to a place you actively recommend?
- ▶ What lessons can you apply to your own business?
- ▶ What traits, habits, or standards from the best companies can you bring into your own customer experience?

Take the time to fill out the grid on the next page and seriously walk through this exercise. The insights you gain won't just change how you see other businesses. They can change how you serve your own customers. And that's where the real magic happens.

	LOYAL	NOT LOYAL
SATISFIED		
NOT SATISFIED		

CHAPTER THREE

THE BOOK OF MASTERS

"If we have 99% [market] share of an industry, the question to us is 'How do we improve the customer satisfaction in order to get that additional 1% share?"

- **Michael Dell**

THE COMPANIES THAT DO IT RIGHT

Some of the most legendary customer service programs aren't just theories — they are lived experiences that have transformed businesses and industries. Let's look at a handful:

The Seattle Fish Market: The FISH! Philosophy

The world-famous Pike Place Fish Market in Seattle isn't just about selling fish. It's about creating an unforgettable experience for customers.

Farrell's Ice Cream: Give 'Em the Pickle

Farrell's Ice Cream Parlour built a legendary reputation on personalized service and a team-driven approach to delighting customers. Founder Bob Farrell's "Give 'Em the Pickle" philosophy reminds businesses that small, thoughtful gestures can make all the difference.

The Ritz-Carlton (Hospitality & Travel)

The Ritz-Carlton sets the standard for luxury service, empowering employees to create memorable, personalized experiences. Their "ladies and gentlemen serving ladies and gentlemen" approach ensures guests feel genuinely valued.

Zappos (E-commerce & Retail)

Zappos is known for obsessive customer service, with stories of representatives spending hours ensuring customers find the perfect item, even if it means directing them to a competitor. Their hassle-free return policy builds long-term trust.

Chewy (Pet Industry & E-commerce)

Chewy's empathetic approach to service includes handwritten notes, condolence cards for lost pets, and surprise gifts for loyal customers. Their human-centered service model makes them one of the most beloved brands in e-commerce.

Alaska Airlines (Air Travel & Transportation)

Alaska Airlines consistently ranks as one of the best U.S. airlines for customer satisfaction. They focus on friendly service, proactive communication, and policies that prioritize passengers over profits, like offering price adjustments if fares drop after booking.

Navy Federal Credit Union (Banking & Finance)

Navy Federal excels in personalized service, easy dispute resolution, and strong customer advocacy, making them one of the most trusted financial institutions, particularly for military families.

Nordstrom (Luxury Retail & Fashion)

Nordstrom is legendary for its customer-first mentality, famously allowing returns with no receipt and empowering employees to go above and beyond for shoppers. Their personalized service and attention to detail set them apart in the retail industry.

Les Schwab Tires (Automotive & Service Industry)

Les Schwab may be regional (Pacific Northwest), but their "We come to you" mentality, free tire checks, and no-appointment-needed service have created a customer service culture that competitors envy. Employees literally run to customers' cars — a physical embodiment of putting service first.

REI (Outdoor & Sporting Goods Retail)

REI's customer-friendly return policies and expert staff make them a leader in retail. Their co-op model fosters trust and community, focusing on long-term customer relationships over quick sales.

Patagonia (Apparel & Sustainability-Focused Retail)

Patagonia is built on service with a mission — offering free product repairs instead of upselling new items and ensuring every customer feels part of a larger environmental movement.

Firehouse Subs (Fast Food & Quick Service Restaurants)

Firehouse Subs stands out in the fast-food industry for genuine hospitality, high-quality ingredients, and a strong community focus. Their commitment to first responders through the Firehouse Subs Public Safety Foundation adds to their reputation for community care.

Costco

Costco isn't just known for low prices — it's known for treating people right. Employees stay for decades because they're paid well, promoted from within, and respected. That loyalty shows up at the registers, in the aisles, and even out in the parking lot. The service is fast, the staff is calm, and customers keep coming back — not just for the deals, but for the way they're treated. As an added bonus, they sample like crazy!

The best companies don't just solve problems — they build long-term customer loyalty through trust, empathy, and consistent excellence.

Whether it's a luxury hotel, a fast-food chain, or a tire shop, the common thread is a commitment to putting people first. Success follows.

THE "TIPPING" POINT – LITERALLY!

Tipping was once a way to reward exceptional service — a little extra given "To Insure Promptness" (T.I.P.). It was a gesture of appreciation, not an obligation. Over time, tipping has evolved from something extra to something expected, and in many cases, even demanded.

Until recently, 15% was the standard tip for good service. Now, the baseline has crept up to 18% or more, with some establishments automatically adding gratuity to the bill and still expecting an additional tip on top of that. Some businesses even present pre-set tipping options starting at 20% or higher, making customers feel pressured into tipping more than they might have otherwise. (We have all seen the card reader with the "extra questions" at the end of the transaction. "It's going to ask you a couple of questions, but of course, there is no obligation…" Of course not!)

This shift in focus has led to contention. Some feel that tipping should still reflect the quality of service, while others believe it's simply part of modern business culture. In many states, certain jobs are classified as "tipped positions," which allows employers to pay below minimum wage while taxing employees on their expected tips. This only fuels the debate: Is tipping a fair way to reward service, or has it become an unfair burden on customers?

Regardless of where you stand on the issue, one fact remains: Your customer service directly impacts your tip. If your income relies on tipping, the best strategy is to deliver exceptional service — every time.

- The better you serve your customers, the better your tip potential.
- If your service is poor, expect lower tips (or none at all).

- Worrying about non-tippers won't help. Making great service a habit will.

If your income is based on tips and you work as a server at a restaurant, it might seem logical that taking on more tables will lead to higher earnings. For example, if you're assigned eight tables but believe you can realistically handle twelve, it may seem like an easy way to increase your income. However, be cautious. Spreading yourself too thin can impact the quality of service you provide, which in turn could affect the tips you receive. While maximizing efficiency is important, there's a fine balance between covering more ground and maintaining excellent service. If quality decreases, the strategy of *more is better* may become ineffective.

Tipping culture may continue to change, but one thing stays the same: Customers tip more when they feel valued. The best way to maximize your earning potential is simple. Wow them with outstanding service every single time.

TRANSPARENCY: THE BALANCING ACT

Transparency in customer service is a delicate balance. You don't need to share every detail of the process, especially when challenges arise. However, keeping customers informed builds trust, maintains control, and strengthens the relationship. Customers feel reassured when they know you're actively working on their issue. Be cautious! Too much transparency can create unrealistic expectations.

For example, if you go too far to the edge of company policies to help a customer and they become aware of it, they may expect special treatment every time. Worse, you could gain a reputation as a rule-breaker, even if you aren't one. As the saying goes, "Perception is 90% of reality."

Here's an example of my own excesses:

Many companies require all calls to employees to go through a central switchboard. (Have you ever called a doctor's office and spoken directly to the doctor?) In one instance, I was concerned that my customer wouldn't be able to navigate the phone system and might have to leave a message I'll never see. So, against policy, but with the best intentions, I gave them my direct extension. They called back as directed, and we resolved the issue. Done, right?

Wrong.

Oh, the issue was resolved, but a few months later, they had another problem. Instead of calling the main line and waiting in the queue like everyone else, they called me directly! Now, they had their own personal representative who could bypass the system. When I told my boss, she just chuckled and said, "Well, that's your problem now." But she also reminded me why the policy existed in the first place.

I eventually redirected the customer back to the proper process, but it was a lesson learned. My transparency, which initially seemed like great customer service, ended up creating an unintended problem. Sometimes, well-meaning exceptions can lead to bigger problems down the road.

That said, keeping the customer involved in the process can be a game-changer. It shows them they are in the hands of a competent expert, allowing them to relax and trust that their issue is being resolved.

SHE WILL BE FINE!

I once had a student in my contact center training class who was terrified of taking her first call. When she finally did, she did so with a more senior agent on the line to guide her. That was the process, and on this day, the assignment. The customer told her of the problem, and she graciously repeated the problem to ensure she heard correctly and told him, "I think I have the solution to that, but I want to make sure I have the right one." She then politely asked to put the customer on hold, turned to her mentor, and whispered, "Do you know what the hell he's even talking about?" Her mentor had the step-by-step resolution pulled up and walked her through it in 10 seconds. She confidently took the customer off hold, followed the process flawlessly, and graciously and very professionally resolved the issue. The customer was delighted!

That moment changed everything. In just a few months, she went from nervous rookie to seasoned pro, earning consistent customer compliments for her confidence and compassion. The key? She kept customers informed and engaged, allowing them to feel like part of the solution.

The Seattle Fish Market is famous for its energy, flying fish, and lively calls across the market floor. They have a simple philosophy: "You have to let the customer in on the fun." When customers feel included, they are always happier.

The same applies in customer service. When customers feel informed and involved, they are more satisfied, more confident in their abilities, and more likely to return.

"KETCHUP" VS. "ketchup"

One is a simple condiment, a small but important detail that enhances a meal. The other? A metaphor for how a single misstep, no matter how small, can overshadow an entire experience.

Imagine this: You have an important job interview scheduled for 11:00 a.m. You arrive early, dressed professionally and fully prepared, only to be told, apologetically, of course, that the interview has been rescheduled to 1:00 p.m. due to a corporate emergency. Understanding, but now with two hours to fill, you head to a nearby restaurant for lunch.

As you sit down to eat, you reach for the ketchup. Just as you're applying it to your burger, someone accidentally bumps into you, causing a bright red splotch to land squarely on your crisp, clean shirt. Panic sets in. You rush to the restroom, scrubbing at the stain with hand soap, paper towels, and sheer determination. No luck. The stain remains, faint but noticeable.

Fast forward to 1:00 p.m. You shake it off, walk into your interview, and absolutely nail it. You're articulate, confident, and qualified. Later, when the hiring team sits down to discuss your interview performance, one person says, "I just couldn't stop focusing on that ketchup stain." Suddenly, your flawless answers and impressive résumé and perfect interview take a backseat to a small, unfortunate distraction.

FIRST IMPRESSIONS...

This is exactly what Chef Robert Irvine, host of *Restaurant: Impossible*, highlights when revamping struggling restaurants. One of the first things he examines is *first impressions*. (Curb appeal, cleanliness, and atmosphere.) A seafood restaurant with old carpeting that traps odors? That's a "ketchup stain." A dining room where tables wobble or the windows are smudged? Another "ketchup stain." These seemingly minor details shape a customer's entire experience before they even take a bite. He spends a lot of time and effort, much to the dismay of his design team, to cover up some of that to enhance the dining experience. He hates an exposed ATM machine. The drink station needs to be behind something. All those elements are important, but not something the customer needs to see. We love transparency, but not that much transparency.

This morning, I noticed a McDonald's drive-thru doing it right. A landscaping crew was tidying the entrance, employees were washing the glass doors, and every team member wore a nametag while keeping personal conversations quiet and professional. The only ketchup I saw? Neatly packed in individual packets, exactly where it belonged.

Small details matter. If a business shows customers that *presentation and experience* are a priority, those customers will be far more likely to return. Because in customer service, you never want the thing people remember most... to be the ketchup stain.

SOMETIMES, FIRST IMPRESSIONS ARE CORRECT

I needed a mobile mechanic due to an electrical issue with my car, and after searching online, I found two options. I went with the one who had the most "thumbs up" reviews. Let's call him Don. Don was scheduled to arrive at a specific time, but arrived approximately an hour late. Turns out, he was coming from three hours away — something I wasn't aware of when I booked him. He pulled up in a Ford Expedition identical to mine, but the moment he opened the back, my confidence wavered. His tools weren't in any kind of toolbox or organized system; they were just tossed in there like a junk drawer on wheels.

Then, things got worse. He grabbed a random handful of tools, took off his shirt, and threw on a backwards hat with borderline offensive language on it. "I need to grab an alternator," he told me, and disappeared for two hours. When I checked outside, my driveway was covered in scattered tools — it was a complete mess. Eventually, he buttoned everything up, charged me the quoted price (cash only, of course), and left. The only problem? The car wasn't fixed.

When I called Don to let him know the car was still not working, he was already four hours away and asked me to test a few things myself. That's when I decided I wasn't about to play mechanic with a multimeter. I needed a real professional. I called the other guy. Enter Jared.

Jared arrived within an hour, driving a clean van with his name and logo on the side. He stepped out wearing a jacket with his name embroidered on it, and when he opened the back of his van, I immediately knew I had made the wrong choice the first time. Everything was neatly arranged, and he exuded professionalism before he even touched my car. Without badmouthing Don, he pointed out that the alternator was still faulty and suggested I return it for a refund. He pointed out that sometimes a faulty part comes right out of the box. While I tracked down Don to get that sorted, Don argued with me. Apparently, I had broken some "unwritten rule" by not calling him first to let him know the part had failed. I reminded him that I wasn't in the habit of throwing good money after bad. I wanted to know how he could have left without retesting the fact that the part replacement he had done, in fact, worked! (but I was nice. I didn't ask that!)

To Don's credit, he did finally help arrange for the return, and I got my money back for that part, but he was more upset with me for not calling him first and bringing in another mechanic than concerned about the fact that my car was still broken. Meanwhile, Jared installed the new alternator in about two hours, charged me $100 less than Don had, and even let me pay by check. The car worked perfectly, and I haven't called anyone else for mechanical work since.

Just like with the ketchup stain analogy, my gut feeling was right from the start. The first impression told me everything I needed to know.

▶ **Reflect on Outstanding Service**

Think about the companies highlighted in this chapter that exemplify outstanding customer service. What do they do differently? Whether it's Zappos' obsessive customer service, The Ritz-Carlton's personalized experiences, or Farrell's Ice Cream's team-driven, fun approach, what practices can you adopt or adapt for your business to improve customer experience?

▶ **Implement the FISH! Philosophy**

Consider the principles behind The Seattle Fish Market's FISH! Philosophy. How can you incorporate these principles into your business? Think about how you and your team can approach customer interactions with more positivity, playfulness, and engagement.

▶ **Create Memorable Experiences**

How can you make someone's day? Like Farrell's Ice Cream, small gestures such as a personal note, offering something extra, a free sundae, singing Happy Birthday, or exceeding customer expectations can build loyalty. What simple changes can you implement to delight your customers and leave a lasting impression?

▶ **Master the Balance of Transparency.**

Transparency in customer service is important, but it's also a balancing act. Take a moment to evaluate how you manage customer expectations. Are you keeping customers informed while avoiding over-promising or creating unrealistic expectations? Think about how you can communicate with your customers in a way that builds trust without crossing the line into over-sharing.

▶ **Embrace the Power of Teamwork.**

Just as Costco emphasizes teamwork in creating great service, how can you ensure your team works together effectively to enhance customer experience? Empower your team to go above and beyond in service. What initiatives or practices can you introduce to foster collaboration and a customer-first mindset among your team? Are your very best practices shared amongst your team?

▶ **Consider the Tipping Culture.**

Reflect on the culture of tipping discussed in the chapter. Whether you're in a business that relies on tips or not, the idea remains: customers reward great service. How can you incentivize exceptional service in your business? Is there a way to make your employees feel more empowered to deliver stellar service, knowing they are helping to earn positive customer recognition?

▶ **Focus on Personalization and Human-Centered Service**

Think about the businesses, like Chewy and Nordstrom, that provide personalized experiences. What steps can you take to make your service more human-centered and tailored to individual customers? What can you do to make each customer feel valued and unique, whether through personalized messages, remembering their preferences, or creating special experiences just for them?

▶ **What is your first impression?**

Is there any Ketchup out there that can be easily fixed

CHAPTER FOUR

THE BOOK OF EMPATHY

"If there is any one secret of success, it lies in the ability to get the other person's point of view and see things from his angle as well as your own."

- **Henry Ford**

THE CUSTOMER'S PERSPECTIVE

Customers don't typically reach out when everything is going smoothly. They come to us because of a problem. Some may be calm, while others might already be frustrated. How we respond in those crucial first moments can determine whether the interaction becomes a partnership or a confrontation.

Ignoring their frustration can quickly escalate the situation into an adversarial encounter. On the other hand, a touch of empathy can shift the dynamic. As that great philosopher Mary Poppins once said, "A Spoonful of Sugar makes the medicine go down!" Acknowledging their frustration without feeding into it too much creates an environment where they feel heard, understood, and supported.

It's essential to strike a balance. Too much sympathy can drain us emotionally, leading to unnecessary stress, whereas practicing empathy allows us to stay engaged without becoming overwhelmed. When we empathize, we're not just problem-solvers. We become partners in their success. This approach helps resolve the issue more effectively and strengthens customer trust and loyalty.

Empathy isn't just about understanding. It's about showing customers they're heard, valued, and supported. The right words can turn frustration into trust, problems into partnerships, and complaints into loyalty.

EMPATHY EXAMPLES:

Retail & Grocery

"My apologies, we just rearranged the store, and I know that can be frustrating. That item is now in Aisle 5. Can I take you there?"

"I completely understand. Running out of something you need is never fun. We'll have more in stock on Thursday. Would you like me to reserve one for you?"

Contact Center & Phone Support

"I hear how frustrating this must be. Let's work together to get this resolved right now."

"I get why this caught you off guard. Let me look into this and find the best solution for you."

Hospitality (Hotels, Restaurants, Travel)

"I completely understand that a delayed check-in can be frustrating. Let me offer you a drink while I get an update on your room."

"I know how disappointing it is when a reservation doesn't go as planned. Let's see how I can make this right for you."

"Travel delays are the worst. I'd be frustrated too. Let's figure out the best alternative together."

Healthcare & Medical Offices

"I can see that you're in discomfort, and I want to make sure you are seen as soon as possible."

"Waiting can be frustrating, especially when you're not feeling your best. I appreciate your patience. I'll check on your appointment status now."

"I hear that this diagnosis is overwhelming. You're not alone, and we're here to help you every step of the way."

Tech Support & IT Helpdesk

"I know how frustrating tech issues can be, especially when you need something just to work. Let's troubleshoot this together."

"I completely understand why this is urgent for you. I'll prioritize this and update you as soon as possible."

"No worries! This happens more often than you'd think. I'll walk you through the fix step by step."

Automotive (Car Dealerships, Repair Shops, Rental Services)

"I know unexpected car issues can throw off your whole day. Let's get this taken care of as quickly as possible."

"I understand. Waiting on repairs is never fun. Let me check the status and see how we can speed things up."

"I'd be frustrated too if my rental wasn't ready on time. Let me see how I can make this right for you."

Banking & Financial Services

"I know how concerning an unexpected charge can be. Let me look into this and make sure we get it resolved."

"I understand that finances can be stressful. Let's review your options together so you feel confident moving forward."

"I can imagine how unsettling it is to see an account issue. I'm here to help, and we'll get this sorted out together."

Empathy isn't just a customer service skill. It's the bridge between frustration and resolution, between a problem and a partnership. We create trust, loyalty, and lasting relationships by acknowledging customers' emotions and guiding them toward a solution with understanding. The right words, tone, and actions can transform a negative experience into a moment of genuine connection. By practicing authentic empathy, we solve problems and help people feel heard, valued, and supported. And that is the foundation of truly exceptional customer service.

BECOMING A BETTER CUSTOMER

Here's something you might not have considered. You may even find yourself becoming a better customer. Think about it: when we discussed empathy, we asked you to see things from the customer's perspective. But what if we flipped the script? What if, when *you* are the customer, you take a moment to consider the person serving you?

I'm not saying you shouldn't be upset when the situation warrants it. However, in my experience, being firm but polite gets better results even when I feel wronged. I've also found that I get more serious attention when I get quieter rather than louder. It may be true that the squeaky wheel gets the grease, but the calm, steady wheel is the one that actually gets you home.

A little kindness goes a long way. In the upcoming *Ten Commandments* section, we'll talk about how small gestures can make a big impact on customer interactions. The same applies when you're on the other side of the counter. A professional, courteous customer is far more likely to receive professional, courteous service in return.

I was reminded of this while leaving Costco one day. There's a long wall inside lined with advertisements for home remodeling services, and usually, there's a rep standing there handing out flyers. Now, let's be honest — not many people walk out of Costco thinking, "You know what? I should sign up for new doors and windows right now!" But I noticed the guy standing there, smiling, trying his best to engage with shoppers who were more focused on getting to their cars.

I didn't need his services, but I stopped for a second and said, 'I'm not in the market for remodeling right now, but I'll give you a fist bump for being out here today. Thanks for the hard work." His reaction? Pure shock — happy shock. He wasn't expecting to be acknowledged, let alone appreciated, just for standing there with a good attitude.

Be a better customer, and you'll get better service. Simple as that. It works both ways.

PUTTING IT TO PRACTICE

▶ **Start with Active Listening.**
For one full day, practice repeating back key concerns in your own words before offering a solution.

▶ **Empathy in Practice: Create Custom Responses.**
Write down three common customer complaints your business receives. Develop empathetic response scripts for each, ensuring they validate the customer's frustration while moving toward a solution. Train yourself or your team to use these scripts in real interactions.

▶ **Empower Your Team to Be Empathetic.**
Schedule a 15-minute team meeting this week to discuss the role of empathy in customer service. Use real examples and conduct a quick role-playing exercise where team members practice handling a frustrated customer with empathy. Then, ask each team member to share one strategy they'll apply immediately.

▶ **Turn the Tables: Be a Better Customer.**
Write down one positive customer service experience you had and identify what made it feel empathetic. Can you apply that to your own business?

CHAPTER FIVE

THE TEN COMMANDMENTS OF CUSTOMER SERVICE

"At a car dealership, the person who sells the car is the hero, and also gets the commission. But if the mechanics don't service that car well, the customer won't return."

- **Roger Staubach**

THE TEN COMMANDMENTS OF CUSTOMER SERVICE

In the beginning, there was Service, and it was good.
Then came Metrics, and Targets, and Endless Quotas.
And lo, they did multiply: calls per hour, seconds per greeting, tickets closed before truly resolved, people waiting endlessly in line, service levels.
The Customer, once sacred, became a stat.
And those on the front lines, those weary warriors of goodwill, were told: "Go faster. Say more. Mean less."

But service was not born from speed, nor from volume.
It came from listening, solving, and leaving people better than you found them.
One customer helped well is worth ten hurried through.

So sayeth the gospel of human decency:
Let us choose Quality over Quantity and rebuild what we've broken.

Not louder. Not cheaper. Not faster.

Better.

As these concepts come together, we need a simple and visual way to show how they apply to any business. We broke them into ten easy principles, which I call the *Ten Commandments of Customer Service*. I'd be willing to bet that as you go through each of them, you'll find at least one area where a slight improvement could make a big difference in your customer's experience.

THE ROAD TO CUSTOMER LOYALTY

Picture driving on a highway towards customer loyalty, with ten crucial exits where customers might choose to leave for better prices, products, or experiences.

Following the Ten Commandments of Customer Service helps you turn customers into lifelong fans and avoid losing them to competitors. As other businesses lose customers, your path becomes clearer and faster, giving you a competitive edge. Keep customers loyal by ensuring they stay on track.

And here's how we do it.

Commandment One: Be Nice. Be Kind. Be Respectful

Being kind, respectful, and sincere costs nothing, but it can have a huge impact on customer satisfaction. It's the foundation for building trust, creating loyalty, and delivering excellent service.

Commandment Two: Be Awesome

Being awesome goes beyond just having a good attitude. It's about confidence, continual learning, professionalism, and finding solutions even when you don't have all the answers. Customers notice when you go the extra mile, and they will remember your efforts. When you bring your best to the table, your customers notice, and that makes a lasting impression.

Commandment Three: Be Present

Give the customer your undivided attention. This means *actively listening* to their concerns, focusing on the conversation, and avoiding distractions. When customers feel heard and valued in the moment, it creates a deeper connection and ensures that their needs are addressed in real time.

Commandment Four: Be Positive

A positive attitude is contagious. By staying upbeat, even in difficult situations, you can diffuse tension and create a better experience for you and the customer. Maintaining optimism helps you handle obstacles with a solution-oriented mindset and inspires confidence in the people you serve.

Commandment Five: Be Sincere. Lend an Ear.

Sometimes, all a customer needs is someone to listen. Showing genuine empathy and understanding builds trust and creates a more personal connection. Listen with your heart, not just your ears, and make sure you're offering real solutions, not just surface-level responses.

Commandment Six: Be Clear. Communicate Well

Communication is at the core of exceptional customer service. Whether dealing with language barriers, speech impairments, or different communication styles, the ability to listen, adapt, and respond effectively makes all the difference. Writing skills, body language, and verbal clarity all play a role in how we connect with others. The best communicators actively seek opportunities to improve. This can be achieved through feedback, structured groups, or real-world practice. Ultimately, refining communication skills isn't just about professional success but about building trust, improving relationships, and creating loyal customers.

Commandment Seven: Be Resolute. Work Towards Closure

Working toward closure means ensuring every customer interaction moves efficiently toward resolution. Customers seek solutions, not endless conversations, so setting clear expectations, respecting their time, and committing to follow-through builds trust and loyalty. When you proactively guide customers toward a resolution and confirm their satisfaction, you elevate their experience and leave a lasting positive impression.

Commandment Eight: Be Open. Give Credence to Complaints

Feedback is a gift. Whether positive or constructive, welcoming feedback shows that you're open to improving and genuinely care about the customer's experience. Use it to learn and grow for yourself and your business. Customer complaints should never be ignored. They offer valuable insights for improvement. By tracking recurring issues, responding promptly, and ensuring a clear resolution process, businesses can turn complaints into opportunities to build trust and loyalty.

Commandment Nine: Be Welcoming. Create an Inviting Work Environment.

A great customer experience starts with an inviting workplace. Employees who enjoy their work create a positive atmosphere that customers notice. By fostering teamwork, balancing structure with flexibility, and encouraging innovation, businesses can build a dynamic environment that keeps both employees and customers coming back. A customer can sense employees under pressure. It does not make them feel at ease.

Commandment Ten: Be Memorable. The Cherry on Top

Going the extra mile doesn't have to be huge — it's about providing more value than expected, whether a small compliment, an added service, or a follow-up to ensure satisfaction. Offering more shows that you genuinely care about the customer and their experience.

These ten commandments form a customer service philosophy about providing value, staying positive, and creating genuine connections with every interaction. By focusing on these principles, you'll provide a fantastic experience for your customers and create a work environment that's fulfilling and motivating.

CHAPTER SIX
COMMANDMENT ONE

BE NICE. BE KIND.
BE RESPECTFUL.

"Be Kind, for everyone you meet is fighting a hard battle."

- **Gloria Vanderbilt**

A TOUCH OF KINDNESS IS ALWAYS REWARDED

Really! It's that easy?! (Just ask the Geek Squad — this is their #1 value.)

The simplest way to build trust with your customers is to show them that you care. It all starts with being nice, kind, and respectful. These may seem like basic principles, but they lay the foundation for every great customer interaction. A smile, a respectful tone, and showing genuine interest in a customer's needs can make all the difference in turning a one-time visitor into a loyal customer.

Small gestures of kindness often mean more than big promises. Developing a rapport with your customers is the simplest way to help them *and* to enjoy your job at the same time. A warm, friendly approach makes all the difference.

Listen carefully.

Do you truly understand what the customer is asking?

Never underestimate the power of "Please" and "Thank you." These small words carry considerable weight in customer interactions. They show that you respect the customer and appreciate their time, making them feel valued.

Think about places with terrible customer service. The DMV comes to mind! Imagine how much better the experience would be if their employees did nothing different except be just a little nicer.

TREAT OTHERS AS YOU WOULD WANT TO BE TREATED

We learned this as kids. It's a core principle in most religions and a guiding value for people across all walks of life. But take it a step further — ask yourself this:

Would you tolerate being treated exactly the way you're treating your customers?

The answer to that question should always be a resounding "Yes!" If you wouldn't accept poor service for yourself, why would you offer it to someone else?

Show that you genuinely care. Sincerity goes a long way. Acknowledge the customer's frustration and always be willing to resolve the issue together.

Remember, you are not the product. You are the bridge between the customer and what they came for. It's your job to guide them toward the solution they're seeking with a respectful and kind demeanor.

Don't take offense if you must apologize for something outside your control. A simple, empathetic response like:

"I'm so sorry you had to go through that — I wouldn't like it either. Let's see what we can do now to make it right"

… keeps the focus on the solution rather than the problem.

Since the pandemic, we've seen both sides of the customer service experience change, and not for the better. We saw more apathy, frustration, and entitlement. Customers shouldn't have to hope for good service. It should be a given.

Most customers know that being rude won't help their cause, but at the end of the day, they are the boss. Some people, like "Joe," won't always be nice, but it makes an impact when you are. During tough times, grateful and enthusiastic service stands out more than ever.

Be nice. Be kind. Be respectful.

It's the easiest way to create a great customer experience. And it costs you nothing.

NAVIGATING TITLES AND FORMALITY IN CUSTOMER INTERACTIONS

It's clear that we have become much less formal than we were 25 years ago. As someone who technically falls into the "baby boomer" category, I was taught that while many titles were assumed rather than earned, some titles do require recognition and respect.

The trend today leans toward first-name interactions, and I largely agree with this shift because it tends to foster a good rapport. However, you can't assume a first-name basis is always welcome. My general approach is to start with either "Mr.," "Miss," "Mrs.," or "Ms.," or when appropriate, the full first and last name.

For example, I might begin a conversation by saying:

"Am I speaking to Robert Jones?"
"Yes, this is Bob."
"Great. Nice to meet you, Bob."

This approach allows the customer to set the tone of the interaction.

If, during the conversation, I learn that the customer has an *earned title*, I immediately adopt it until I am corrected.

Clergy Titles: If I confirm someone is a member of the clergy, I use their title unless directed otherwise. *Example:*

> "Are you Monsignor Murphy?"
> *"Yes, but people call me Father Tim."*
> At that point, I shift to "Father Tim."

Doctors:

This is the title I am most sensitive to. If I see MD, DMD, DDS, PhD, EdD, DO, etc. in documents or hear it in conversation, I immediately use "Doctor" or "Doc." About half the time, the customer will correct me with a preference for something less formal, and I always defer to their choice. Doctors tend to want the title they have earned.

Military Titles:

If I find out someone is a veteran or retired military, I make an effort to acknowledge their service. For example, if a person retired as a Navy E7, I may ask if I can call them "Chief" as a sign of respect. This applies to any known military rank.

Note: If you are not familiar with Military ranks, please do not go here. It is a nice touch, but not necessary, and it can cause problems in the wrong situations if done incorrectly. If you work at a military PX or for USAA, defer to their training, but take the time to learn.

Overly Casual Addressing: What to Avoid

While I aim to be approachable, there are certain overly casual forms of address that I find unprofessional, especially in a first interaction. These include:

- "Honey" or "Hun"
- "Dude"
- "Boss"
- "Hey, You"

- "'Sup, Dog!'"

Being called by my initials (unless I insist)

In casual settings, I may use "Hello, Friend" as a warm but professional greeting, but that's about as informal as I get.

SIR AND MA'AM: A CHANGING PERCEPTION

I was taught that "Sir" and "Ma'am" were signs of respect. However, these days, some people perceive them as making them "sound old" or outdated. If you use these terms and sense discomfort, you can quickly apologize and ask if they'd prefer their first name. The key is sincerity — most people appreciate an effort to adjust. Personally, I am fine with it.

Since company policies on this can vary, it's wise to check with your HR team to see if there are any official guidelines. You may not believe this, but companies now have established policies around this.

Using titles and understanding levels of formality can be a tipping point for building great rapport. If you get it wrong, the key is to adjust gracefully, making the interaction a positive experience regardless. The goal is to make the customer feel comfortable and respected throughout the conversation.

PUTTING IT TO PRACTICE:

▶ **Greet Every Customer Warmly.**
Make eye contact, smile, and acknowledge each customer immediately — whether in person, on the phone, or online. For the next week, consciously greet each customer within five seconds of engagement.

▶ **Use "Please" and "Thank You" in Every Interaction.**
These words set the tone for a respectful exchange. If you are not already doing so, challenge yourself to use "please" and "thank you" with each customer interaction.

▶ **Pause Before Reacting to Frustration.**
If a customer is upset, take a deep breath before responding. Focus on helping, not defending. Next time you feel defensive, silently count to three before answering with empathy and a solution.

▶ **End Every Interaction on a Positive Note.**
No matter how the conversation starts, leave the customer with a positive experience. Before ending an interaction, say something like *"I appreciate you choosing us today. Let me know if you need anything else."*

CHAPTER SEVEN

COMMANDMENT TWO

BE AWESOME

"Well done is better than well said."

— **Benjamin Franklin**

THE ONGOING QUEST FOR EXCELLENCE

Being awesome isn't just about having a great attitude — it's about continual learning, professionalism, and confidence in your role. Customers can tell when they're dealing with someone who knows their stuff, and that confidence puts them at ease. But remember — there's a fine line between confidence and arrogance. Stay humble, stay curious, and always strive to be better.

ALWAYS KEEP LEARNING

The best service professionals never stop improving. No matter what industry you're in:

Learn what goes on in other departments.

The more you understand the big picture, the better you can assist customers.

Expand your knowledge of products and services.

Be the one who can answer, "Do you carry this?" with a solution, not a shrug.

Seeking out new skills.

Attend workshops, take courses, or shadow an expert. If you're not the go-to person in your area, find out who they are and learn from them.

Develop resources. Know where to get answers when you don't have them on hand. Customers appreciate effort more than empty answers.

FIND WAYS TO BUILD RAPPORT

Rapport isn't just for salespeople but for anyone who interacts with customers. Small talk, finding common ground, and making genuine connections can turn an average interaction into a memorable one.

You don't need hours to build rapport — you can do it in seconds.

If you're a cashier at Home Depot, a simple *"Wow, that looks like an ambitious project!"* can spark engagement.

You already know if you're in sales: *No rapport, no sale.* People buy from people they like and trust.

Look for opportunities everywhere — a shared interest, a compliment, or even just using a customer's name. When you take a moment to connect, customers pay attention.

KNOW WHAT YOU TRULY OFFER

It's easy for a business to assume they know what makes customers choose them, but the truth is, what you think you offer and what customers value can be very different.

Take this real-life example:

In the late 1970s, an oil company entered the automobile gasoline market with a bold strategy. They developed a refining formula that produced the highest-octane fuel at the most competitive price. Naturally, they expected drivers to flock to their stations.

They didn't.

Confused by the lack of sales, the company surveyed both loyal customers and those who had taken their business elsewhere. They asked a simple question:

"What is the most important factor when choosing a gas station while traveling?"

> Was it high-quality fuel?
> Better pricing?
> More convenient locations?
> Excellent service?

Nope. It was *clean bathrooms*.

Drivers weren't just looking for gas — they needed a clean, comfortable stop along the way. Without realizing it, the company wasn't really in the gasoline business; they were in the clean bathroom business.

Once they prioritized spotless restrooms, sales and customer loyalty immediately increased.

No matter what business you're in, understand what your customers value most and deliver on that.

THE RIGHT TOOLS FOR THE JOB

A golf pro wouldn't dream of entering a tournament with rented clubs. You shouldn't approach your job without the right tools either.

Invest in quality tools that make you more efficient and improve customer experience. Think about what a Home Depot associate keeps in their apron — useful gadgets, tape measures, radios, calculators — all things that help the customer faster and better.

With time and experience comes confidence. When you're confident in what you do, customers will be satisfied with you.

PROFESSIONALISM MATTERS

No matter how much you know, how you present yourself matters just as much:

Dress appropriately.

Your appearance sets the tone before you even speak.

Be on time.

If you commit to something, follow through.

Confirm appointments.

A simple follow-up can save misunderstandings.

Check your work.

Make sure the food is right before handing it out, the order is correct before it ships, and the problem is genuinely solved before you close the case.

Follow up when necessary.

Checking back shows you care beyond the transaction.

As always, "Please" and "Thank you" never go out of style. Stay respectful, stay helpful, and you'll always be awesome.

IT'S NOT JUST ABOUT BEING RIGHT — SOMETIMES IT'S ABOUT GETTING IT RIGHT

Knowing the correct answer in customer service is valuable, but what truly matters is how you handle situations when the answer isn't ideal. Sometimes, you don't have the tools, policies, or ability to solve a customer's problem directly. However, the way you respond in these moments can define the entire interaction.

Excellent service isn't just about having all the answers or about finding solutions, even when the solution isn't in your hands.

A real-world example.

I recently went to the pharmacy to fill a prescription for my son. Not only was the medication out of stock, but it was also on backorder for months. The pharmacist could have said, *"Sorry, we don't have it."* Instead, he went the extra mile. He stepped out from behind the counter and told me he had already called and found another pharmacy within my insurance network with the medication in stock.

Yes, I had to drive across town, but he saved me hours of frustration and potential panic. He turned a *"no"* into a solution.

Even when you can't help, you can still be helpful. Customers remember the effort. If you show that you genuinely care about finding a solution, even if that means directing them to a competitor, you will earn their trust, respect, and future business.

THE PEPPERONI PRINCIPLE

I've heard many military veterans talk about the value of making their bed. Not because it's hard, but because doing it first thing every morning instills discipline. At first, it's a chore. Eventually, it becomes routine and sets the tone for a productive day.

Now, I never had that military experience. But I had a different kind of wake-up call — at 16 years old, on my first day at Pietro's Pizza.

They put me on the line, where I had to build pizzas by the book. Every station was set up for maximum efficiency. You didn't just throw ingredients on randomly; you followed a sequence. Grab, sprinkle, move on. Except for one pizza.

The old-fashioned pepperoni.

Every pizza joint has one. And every pizza joint knows — you don't sprinkle pepperoni. You place it. Slice by slice. Each one slightly overlapping. An 18-inch pie takes time. Even the fastest workers couldn't rush it. But the result? A beautiful pizza. Perfectly balanced. Evenly cooked. Visually appealing.

Sure, people *tried* to cut corners with a sprinkle-and-spread method. But by the time they rearranged everything to look right, they'd lost any time they thought they'd saved.

What I learned was simple: speed might get you a customer once. Quality brings them back.

KEEP LEARNING, STAY AWESOME

The main thing about being awesome — *truly* awesome — is not about being flashy, perfect, or flawless. It's about having the *desire* to keep getting better at what you do. That's it. That's the whole secret.

You can have all the natural talent in the world, but if you stop learning, you stall. The people who seem to thrive the most are the ones who stay curious. They look for new ways to improve. They study their own mistakes. They ask better questions the second time around. That mindset alone sets them apart.

There's a moment in *The Once and Future King* where young King Arthur asks his mentor, Merlin, "What's the secret to not growing old while *getting* old?" And Merlin gives him the best answer ever:

> "The best thing is to learn something. That's the only thing that never fails...
> Learn why the world wags and what wags it. That is the only thing which the mind can never exhaust... Learning is the thing for you."
> – T.H. White, *The Once and Future King*

I think back to when I was sixteen, working the line at the pizza parlor. I wasn't doing anything glamorous — making pizzas, washing dishes, wiping tables, and prepping food. But what I *wanted* was to be one of the guys watching the ovens. (actually cooking the food) *That* was the job. That's what I saw as the top of the mountain, or at least the next step towards it.

One night after the dinner rush, I asked a floor boss, "Can you show me how to do that?" To his credit, he took ten minutes to walk me through it. Step by step. Not just how to do it, but *why it mattered* if we do it right. "Remember," he said, "this is someone's family dinner."

That stuck with me. I wanted to be so good I could do anything. I learned to handle the front of house, back of house, the dishwasher, and whatever we needed. I liked learning the whole place. It took a couple of years, but I eventually got there. And it started with a question: *Can you show me how to do that?*

MANAGING EXPECTATIONS: THE KEY TO CUSTOMER SATISFACTION

Expectations play a critical role in every customer interaction. Following through on promises builds trust, but you must be careful about what you promise in the first place. Overpromising and underdelivering can damage credibility and lead to frustration.

Take, for example, a customer at an automobile tire center asking for an oil change. A poor response would be, "Sure, we can take care of that," only for the customer to find out later that the service isn't offered. Instead, a better approach might be:

"We actually don't do oil changes here, but there are a couple of great spots nearby that many of our customers recommend. Here's where they are."

Even though you didn't get their business, you set the right expectation and still provided value. By knowing your job well and understanding what you can and can't offer, you create a smoother, more positive experience. That alone can turn a one-time interaction into long-term trust.

In customer service, setting the right expectations isn't about always saying 'yes' — it's about being honest, proactive, and helpful. When done correctly, it becomes a bridge to stronger conversations, happier customers, and better relationships.

▶ **Always Keep Learning.**

Never stop improving your skills and knowledge. Learn from other departments, seek out training, and constantly expand your understanding of products and services. What offerings are out there that you might be able to take advantage of soon?

▶ **Build Rapport Quickly.**

Make every customer interaction count. Look for opportunities to connect and create a lasting impression. "That's a great project you're working on. Do you need help finding something to make it easier?"

▶ **Know What You Truly Offer.**

Understand what your customers value most and always deliver on those expectations. Even if it means pointing them to a competitor.

▶ **Use the Right Tools.**

Equip yourself with the tools that make your job easier and help improve customer experience.

▶ **Set and Manage Expectations Like a Pro.**

Practice clear communication and set realistic expectations every time. "Unfortunately, we can't do that, but here's what we can do to resolve this situation."

▶ **Be Professional at All Times.**

Dress appropriately, be on time, and always follow through. Your professionalism will make a lasting impression. "I'll confirm our meeting tomorrow and send over the details right away.

CHAPTER EIGHT
COMMANDMENT THREE

BE PRESENT

"Spend a lot of time talking to customers face-to-face. You'd be amazed how many companies don't listen to their customers."

- **Ross Perot**

NAVIGATING THE WORLD OF DISTRACTIONS

Multitasking is a myth. Science has proven that the brain cannot focus on two things simultaneously. It simply switches rapidly between tasks. And each time it switches, attention and efficiency suffer. Multitasking is the second leading cause of traffic accidents, right behind impaired driving. If it's dangerous on the road, imagine its damage to customer service.

When you are with a customer, be fully there — even if it's only for a brief moment. Give them your undivided attention. Nothing makes a customer feel less valued than sensing they are an afterthought. If you must keep your phone on for emergencies, set that expectation upfront so your customer understands.

Some businesses set employees up for failure by forcing them to split their focus. Imagine a fast-food drive-thru worker who must take new orders on a headset while serving food at the window. You may have encountered this before. It is frustrating for the customer and overwhelming for the employee. Now imagine how exceptional that worker could be if they weren't asked to do two things simultaneously.

This "being present" principle is a core value of Seattle's world-famous Pike Place Fish Market. They understand that when a customer is in front of you, they are your entire world — even just for a few minutes.

GIVE YOUR FULL ATTENTION

Make eye contact and acknowledge the customer immediately.

Put your phone away. No checking messages or scrolling.

Keep waiting time to an absolute minimum. No one likes to wait, so respect their time.

Empathize with customers who've had bad experiences before reaching you. Acknowledge it and do your best to turn things around.

Never give your customer the impression that someone else is more important than they are at that moment. It's not just rude, it's bad business.

THE COST OF NOT "BEING THERE"

A lack of presence in customer service doesn't just lose a single sale; it can cost a business big money in lost loyalty.

A man in dirty coveralls walked into a bank and asked the teller to validate his parking ticket. He explained he had just dropped off a prescription for his wife at the drugstore next door.

The teller responded, "Did you do business in the bank today?"

"No," the man said. "But I have an account here and didn't bring any cash to pay for parking."

"I'm sorry, sir," the teller replied. "But if you didn't do business in the bank today, I can't validate your ticket."

A $5 parking ticket ended up costing the bank significantly.

The next day, the man returned, closed all three accounts (totaling $1.4 million), and canceled his $500,000 credit line. He took his business across the street to a competitor. Small, thoughtless policies can have enormous consequences.

COMMON WAYS BUSINESSES FAIL TO "BE THERE"

Here are a few examples of situations where customers feel ignored or undervalued:

- No shopping carts or baskets available at store entrances.
- Long wait times to place an order or receive food.
- Long checkout lines — or long lines anywhere.
- A store that is frequently out of stock on key items.
- Websites that are outdated, slow, or completely down.
- Improper expectations set for a product or service.
- Businesses close at times when customers need them most.

Would you wait in long lines at checkout if competitors had shorter ones? Would you go to an ice cream shop that closed early on a hot day? Would you return to a business that constantly lacks the products you need?

Customers notice these things. And if you are not "Present," they will find someone who is.

FIND WAYS TO SAY "YES!"

Customers often ask for things outside the standard menu of products and services. The truth is, you won't always be able to give them exactly what they want. But what can you do?

- If there's a workaround, offer it.
- If you genuinely can't help, tell them what you *can* do.
- If necessary, direct them to where they *can* be helped, even if it's a competitor.

Customers don't expect perfection, but they do expect effort. When you go the extra mile, they will remember it.

Being present doesn't just mean physically being there; it means being engaged, focused, and ready to help. Your customers will notice. More importantly, they will return.

NO SANDWICH FOR YOU!

It was supposed to be a simple meal. My wife, my special needs son, and I had walked into a Subway, as we often did, ready for a familiar and easy dining experience. At the time, my son was fixated on one particular food: grilled and toasted cheese sandwiches. This wasn't an unusual request; Subway's entire model is based on customers customizing their own sandwiches right in front of them. It should have been simple.

But it wasn't.

I politely asked the worker if we could have a sandwich made with just bread and a few different cheeses put through the toaster. Immediately, the employee's demeanor shifted. Curt and visibly annoyed, she seemed almost offended that I wasn't ordering directly from the menu. I calmly reiterated my request, explaining that I just wanted a custom sandwich, something I had assumed wouldn't be an issue at a place that literally builds sandwiches to order.

Her response?

"We know how much to charge for the sandwiches on the menu, but not a custom sandwich. Why don't you just order one from the menu?"

I was dumbfounded. This wasn't some obscure, off-the-wall request. I wasn't asking for a five-layer cake or a sushi roll. I was asking for bread, cheese, and a toaster — the most basic sandwich ingredients. Still, she was adamant, and her tone grew even more unpleasant. Realizing that reason wasn't going to get me anywhere, I decided to play by her rigid, illogical rules. I ordered a ham sandwich with multiple types of cheese, just as a workaround. We paid, took our food to the table, and removed the ham ourselves. Problem solved. Or so we thought.

As we ate, I noticed her and her coworkers pointing at us, whispering, and exchanging glances. I had no idea what they were discussing, but their behavior was unprofessional at best. It was enough to make us feel uncomfortable in what should have been a casual dining setting.

Before leaving, I decided to address it.

"Is there a problem?" I asked.

Her response? "In the future, just order a sandwich from the menu."

I couldn't believe it. Rather than simply accommodating a customer with an easy request, she doubled down. So, I asked to talk to her manager.

"I *am* the owner," she said smugly.

That was the final straw. Not only did she lose us as customers, but she ensured that we would never recommend her business to anyone. It wasn't long before I learned she had quite a reputation in town. People called her the "Sandwich Nazi," (a reference to the infamous "Soup Nazi" from *Seinfeld*.) The name fits.

Ultimately, her Subway franchise was closed for good. We later heard it was for poor sales, mismanagement, and employment violations.

And here's the real takeaway. If she had simply taken a moment to be kind, to listen, and to accommodate a simple request, she could have gained a loyal customer. Whenever we visited that neighborhood, which occurred quite often, we would have returned. Instead, she not only lost our business but became the subject of a cautionary tale — one I've told dozens of times. Now, it's in this book as an example of what *not* to do in customer service.

All it would have taken was a little bit of kindness. Instead, she chose stubbornness, and it cost her everything.

HAVE BAG, WILL TRAVEL

When I was refereeing basketball, my commissioner had a phrase: "Have bag, will travel." The idea was to always keep a fully packed bag ready to go in the car, a "go bag" of sorts, even on days when I didn't have a scheduled game. That way, if a last-minute opportunity came up, I was prepared.

This concept applies to many industries. Most jobs require essential tools or supplies to be effective. Contractors and tradespeople often have separate trucks or vans stocked with everything they need to handle most jobs. Many drivers keep emergency tools in their cars for unexpected roadside issues. So why not apply that same level of preparedness to your own business?

For example, in my current role as a mobile notary, I make sure my notary bag is always fully stocked with everything I might need. Each night, I check that it's well-equipped, and every morning, I securely place it in my car. I can't tell you how many times I've received a last-minute call for an appointment while on the road, and was grateful to be ready.

Are there ways you can always be prepared in your own work?

▶ **Acknowledge Immediately**

Greet every customer right away — even if you're busy. Say *"I'll be right with you!"* within 5 seconds of them approaching.

▶ **Ditch the Distractions**

Stay off your phone and avoid side conversations while helping a customer. Keep your device out of sight during work hours unless it's job-related.

▶ **Listen All the Way Through**

Let the customer speak fully before responding. Pause 1–2 seconds after they finish speaking to ensure you've fully heard them.

▶ **Make it Personal**

Show the customer you're focused on *them*, not just the transaction. Use their name if possible, or make one genuine comment based on what they've said.

▶ **Write it Down**

Even if you have a stellar memory, writing things down shows the customer that their words matter. Whether it's an order, an address, a difficult name to pronounce, or a special request, jotting it down signals respect, professionalism, and a commitment to getting it right the first time

CHAPTER NINE
COMMANDMENT FOUR

BE POSITIVE

"It is never wrong to do the right thing."

— **Mark Twain**

BE THE REASON THEIR DAY GETS BETTER

Your attitude is a choice. You decide whether to show up grumpy and disengaged or cheerful and enthusiastic. But here's the secret: A positive attitude improves the job — not just for the customer, but for *you*.

Think about it. You're here anyway. Why not make it enjoyable?

When customers come to you, they usually have a goal in mind. Although there may be frustration, strive to find common ground and assist them in achieving their objectives.

ELIMINATE NEGATIVE LANGUAGE

Words matter. Negative phrases can shut down conversations and leave customers feeling stuck. Instead of saying what can't be done, shift the focus to what *can* be done.

- "We don't have that in stock."
- "That item is super popular! We're expecting more next week, and I'd be happy to set one aside for you."

- "We can't do that."
- "Here's what I can do for you."

- "Oops!"
- "Let me fix that for you right away."

This simple shift builds trust, keeps the conversation moving forward, and often opens the door to sales opportunities.

SET PROPER EXPECTATIONS

Not all news is good news, and customers appreciate honesty. If something can't be done, be upfront about it, but don't dwell on the problem. Shift the focus to solutions.

For example:

- If an order is delayed, provide a realistic timeline instead of false hope.
- If a product isn't available, suggest a suitable alternative. (I recommend several, if I can, so they can choose.)
- If a service isn't offered, direct the customer to someone who can help.

Customers don't expect perfection, but they do expect clear communication and a willingness to help.

Bottom Line: Positivity is Contagious

Your attitude sets the tone for every customer interaction. A solution-focused approach can enhance the customer's experience. It makes your day better, too. Choose positivity and watch how it transforms your work.

It's natural to have frustrations at work, but your customer is not the right audience. When you complain, even in passing, it shifts the focus away from their concerns and makes the interaction about you. That's not what they came for.

Here's a perfect example:

A phone agent once started a customer call already frustrated. They informed the customer that they were frustrated due to being stuck in traffic on a local freeway. But the customer? They were calling from Bethpage, NY. If you know anything about New York traffic, you know that getting stuck on the Long Island Expressway (LIE) makes a local freeway look like a scenic Sunday drive.

The customer's response? "You think you got problems? I can't log onto my computer because the connection is bad. Can we be more concerned about that, please?"

Customers don't call to hear about your bad day. They have their own problems to solve. Keep the focus where it belongs: on them.

Even if you're having a rough day, resist the urge to vent. Instead:

- Acknowledge the customer's frustration.
- Stay professional and engaged.
- Keep the conversation solution-focused.

Your struggles are real, but should never become the customer's problem. Stay present, stay professional, and keep focus on helping them. If the situation is impossible to separate, perhaps you need to step away for a minute or two. Is a break possible? Might you have a confidant at work you can talk to?

Don't let it get to this point.

PETE-ISMS

During my time on the contact center floor, we had a technician I'll call "Pete" (not his real name). He was usually capable, but things quickly went wrong with difficult customers.

Pete had little patience for customers who didn't see the process as a team effort, and when frustration took over, his emotions ran high. His teammates, those seated near his cubicle, began to notice a pattern. Calls would escalate, voices would rise, and his responses would become increasingly sharp and rude. Over time, people stopped trying to ignore it. Instead, they would exchange glances, roll their eyes, or even walk away, unable to listen to how rude, condescending, and dismissive he had become.

It got so bad that his coworkers started compiling a list of his most outrageous remarks. Eventually, the quality assurance team caught wind of it and began monitoring him more closely. Not long after, Pete left the company. His legacy lived on in office folklore. By the way, not surprisingly, the team's quality scores immediately climbed upon his departure. A cautionary tale.

Here are just a few of the most memorable "Pete-isms" from that infamous list (those that I can quote):

- "No, no, no, NO, NO!"
- "You will make this much easier if you stop analyzing everything I do!
- "What part of what I'm telling you do you not understand?"
- "What did you do *that* for?"
- "So, What!?!"
- "Sir, I will repeat it one more time. It is impossible…"
- "Yeah, and…"

Pete may have moved on, but his words remained, repeated in hushed tones, shared with new hires as a cautionary tale, and immortalized in the annals of contact center history.

PUTTING IT TO PRACTICE:

▶ Start each day by setting a positive intention for your interactions.

▶ Identify three common negative phrases you use and replace them with positive alternatives.

▶ When delivering bad news, immediately follow it with a solution or alternative.

▶ Practice using neutral, inclusive language in greetings and interactions.

▶ Before venting at work, ask yourself: "Is this something my customer or teammate needs to hear?"

▶ Take short mental breaks when needed to maintain a positive and professional attitude

CHAPTER TEN
COMMANDMENT FIVE

BE SINCERE

"Most people do not listen with the intent to understand; they listen with the intent to reply."

— **Stephen R. Covey**

LEND AN EAR

Let people vent. Sometimes, the best thing you can do for a customer is simply to listen. Give them space to express their frustrations, concerns, or even excitement, and do so with sincerity. If you need to respond, do so with kindness and empathy.

If you're interacting in person, make eye contact while they speak. If needed, take notes. It shows you are engaged and value what they're saying. A great example is food servers who don't write down orders. (A personal pet peeve of mine.) Even if they have a flawless memory, writing the order down reassures the customer that they are truly being heard, and their request will be accurate.

Minimize interruptions. Allowing customers to fully express themselves builds trust and rapport. Often, they don't necessarily need a solution right away; they just want to know someone is listening.

I learned this lesson the hard way as a basketball referee. In my early years, I was quick to call technical fouls — probably 300 in my first five seasons. I had what many newer officials have, "Rabbit Ears." One day, a senior official I respected saw me call one on a coach, and later, asked what he had said. I told him the coach was barking at me for the entire game, it got very distracting for me, so I rang him up. The truth is, I probably did not know what he said. The complaining came across as "white noise" to me because of the loud nature in which it was being delivered. The official gave me a simple but valuable piece of advice:

"Next time, take an extra beat and actually listen to what he's saying. Find out what he's asking (or complaining) about. It might be relevant and could even disarm him. Certainly, the act of taking a moment to listen can bring the volume level down to a manageable tone, and you could have a conversation."

I realized that sometimes they were just venting, but other times, they were trying to communicate something that could be important. I learned to appreciate that. One might even go so far as to call it "maturity."

That advice stuck with me. Over the next 25 years, I only issued nine technical fouls. Not because coaches stopped yelling, but because I learned to lend an ear. These situations usually de-escalated on their own, and I became a much better and more respected official. I learned to tell the difference between them simply yelling to yell and when they were trying to get an important message across.

The same applies to our customers. When people feel heard, tensions lower, and productive conversations can happen.

This can be a real game-changer. It was for me.

► **Give people space to express themselves.**
Sometimes, they don't need a solution right away — they just want to be heard.

► **Engage fully in the conversation.**
Make eye contact when possible, take notes if needed, and show that you genuinely value what they're saying.

► **Pause and truly listen before reacting.**
Ask yourself: Are they just venting, or is there an important message beneath the frustration?

► **Respond with kindness and empathy.**
A simple acknowledgment of their feelings can go a long way in de-escalating tension.

► **Recognize that listening builds trust.**
When people feel heard, conversations become more productive, and relationships grow stronger.

BE CLEAR

"The first step in exceeding your customer's expectations is to know those expectations."

- **Roy H. Williams**

COMMUNICATE WELL

Much of this book is about communication. We've already covered building rapport, keeping things positive, and active listening. Now, let's focus on listening when listening is difficult.

Some customers may have special needs, speech impairments, or brain diseases, such as strokes or Alzheimer's. Others may have a different primary language, making communication more challenging. I've always regretted not learning a second language, as it's an invaluable tool in customer service. Exceptional writing skills are also essential in most professions — not just contextual writing but also legible handwriting. Many schools no longer teach cursive writing. Writing skills are on the decline, so it's no surprise that Writing 121 is required for all college freshmen. Being concise is a challenge, even for experienced communicators. In fact, about a third of the pages of this book were cut due to redundancy and excessive wordiness.

Communication is part of being awesome. I know some of you may have special needs, such as OCD, Asperger's, an overwhelming nervousness about speaking, or even a neurological disorder such as Tourette's syndrome. That's okay. You may not be interacting with teammates or customers directly, but your ability to formulate clear messaging is still crucial. In an earlier chapter, we discussed "Fred" in the workplace as someone who works behind the scenes. Even if *you* are Fred, your communication directly impacts others. Fred supports Mary, who, in turn, helps Joe.

So, how can you improve your communication skills? Start by joining social groups such as a book club or an activity-based organization where you can meet and interact with people. Toastmasters is an excellent, cost-effective way to develop public speaking and leadership skills in a structured environment with constant feedback at a low cost. Seeking feedback from peers after major projects, or even during them, shows a willingness to improve for a better customer experience.

Another valuable way to gain insight into communication is through "secret shopping." Many companies use secret shoppers to understand what customers genuinely experience versus what the company believes it provides. The results can be eye-opening.

Communication also extends beyond direct interactions. Some jobs require daily, weekly, monthly, quarterly, or annual reports. In the contact center industry, we logged every single call so the next agent could follow the customer's history. Body language tells a large part of the story on a retail floor or in an in-home service setting, such as handyman work or landscaping.

Communication is everywhere. We need to recognize it, refine it, and own it. It can be the difference between a merely satisfied customer and a loyal one.

LET GEORGE DO IT

George Stephanopoulos, co-host of "Good Morning America" and former communications advisor for President Bill Clinton, learned some valuable lessons early in his career. Among them were what he called the "Four C's of Communication." A set of principles designed to ensure effective, impactful, and meaningful interactions.

Clarity – Say What You Mean

Clear communication is about delivering a message that is easily understood. Jargon, ambiguity, or overly complex explanations only create confusion. Whether speaking to a single person or an audience of millions, clarity ensures that the message lands exactly as intended. The best communicators remove unnecessary fluff and focus on what truly matters — getting the point across.

Concision – Get to the Point

Time is valuable, and attention spans are limited. A great communicator trims the excess and delivers a message efficiently. Rambling or over-explaining dilutes the impact of what is being said. The most powerful messages, whether in politics, business, or personal interactions, are often the simplest.

Curiosity – Listen to Understand

The best communicators don't just talk; they listen. Curiosity drives deeper engagement, better questions, and more thoughtful responses. Instead of assuming they have all the answers, strong communicators seek to understand different perspectives, ask insightful questions, and show a genuine interest in the conversation.

Candor – Speak the Truth, Even When It's Hard

Honesty and transparency build trust. Being candid means communicating openly, even when delivering difficult news or admitting mistakes. However, candor should always be paired with tact — brutal honesty without consideration can do more harm than good. A balance of directness and empathy makes messages more credible and impactful.

By mastering these four C's (Clarity, Concision, Curiosity, and Candor), anyone can improve their communication skills, whether in a boardroom, a newsroom, or an everyday conversation.

There is an old joke I hear a lot. "You might not believe this, but I am often accused of being condescending. Condescending means talking down to people."

THE MAZE OF CUSTOMER DIS-SERVICE

At a major online company, a couple of highly publicized security breaches occurred. These incidents happen from time to time, even to the biggest tech firms. In response, the company sent out a reassuring message to customers, advising them to reset their passwords to protect their accounts. For the most part, this was true — except for one major problem.

The password reset process was a nightmare.

What should have been a simple fix turned into a frustrating maze. Customers found themselves trapped in endless loops with the so-called "Password Wizards." Options were either grayed out or missing entirely. Every path seemed broken, and no matter which route customers took, they hit dead ends.

The support team relayed these frustrations to the programming team, but it felt like shouting into the void. No one was paying attention: not the engineers, middle management, or decision-makers. Customers were suffering, and the company was losing them.

Finally, a manager escalated the issue to a VP. Instead of just hearing them out, he took action. He tasked them with designing four straightforward, engineer-approved password reset scenarios that customer service agents could actually use. When other VPs wanted to send their teams to review these scenarios, he insisted they experience the process firsthand. His reasoning? Mid-management had become completely disconnected from the real customer experience.

That meeting changed everything. The VP showed his peers each scenario from the customer's perspective. He had them walk through each scenario with their own computers to see exactly what a mess they were putting their customers through. His colleagues shifted from passive to outraged. They hadn't realized just how broken the process had become. Seeing how many loyal customers were getting frustrated, through no fault of their own, they recognized that the company was making things unnecessarily difficult.

Some executives rushed into the hallway to call their chief engineers. Others ran the same scenarios through their own teams. Even the CEO went through the process. That's when things finally started moving.

Within days, the reset process once again became simple. Instructions were much clearer. Dead links were fixed. What had once been a system bogged down by indifference transformed into one driven by customer focus. Apathy gave way to empathy.

No one knows exactly how many customers were lost in the interim. But one thing became clear. When leadership truly listened, they were finally able to make things right.

This is a perfect example of why listening matters. Customers don't just want solutions. They want to be heard. Every frustration is an opportunity to improve, but only if companies are willing to pay attention.

▶ **Practice patience and active listening.**
Whether dealing with language barriers, speech impairments, or difficult conversations, take time to understand before responding.

▶ **Adapt your communication style.**
Match your tone, clarity, and approach to fit the person or situation, whether in writing or conversation.

▶ **Join groups that strengthen communication skills.**
Consider book clubs, Toastmasters, Meet-ups, or team-based activities to improve public speaking and interpersonal skills.

▶ **Seek feedback to improve.**
Ask colleagues or supervisors how you can refine your speaking, writing, or body language to communicate more effectively.
Do you have a channel for customer feedback that actually gets monitored and actioned?

▶ **Recognize that communication is everywhere.**
Whether through body language, written reports, or casual conversations, clear messaging can turn a one-time interaction into long-term trust.

BE RESOLUTE

"The key is to set realistic customer expectations and then not to just meet them, but to exceed them — preferably in unexpected and helpful ways."

— **Richard Branson**

"BEGIN WITH THE END IN MIND" – (Covey)

One of Stephen Covey's Seven Habits of Highly Effective People is *Begin with the End in Mind.* This principle is just as relevant in customer service as it is in leadership and personal development. When a customer approaches you with a need or a problem, they are looking for a resolution. The key to a great customer service experience is ensuring that every interaction moves toward that resolution efficiently and effectively.

General Colin Powell, known for his strategic military and diplomatic efforts, always emphasized the importance of an exit strategy. He would ask, *"I see why we need to go in, but how do we get out?"* He understood that entering into a situation without a clear path to closure can lead to confusion, inefficiency, and frustration. While this principle may have been applied to global conflicts, the core idea applies just as much to customer interactions, whether in a retail store, contact center, or in the service industry. Every customer conversation should begin with the goal of a clear and satisfactory ending.

Customers come to you because they trust that you have the knowledge and ability to help them. Your job is to ensure that their needs are met in a timely manner so they can move forward. No customer enjoys waiting, and no one wants to feel like their time is being wasted. Keep that checkered flag in sight, the final goal, and work toward it with purpose.

KEY PRINCIPLES OF CLOSURE:

- Show the customer you care about getting it right.
- Assure them you're willing to stay with it until it is done.
- Leave customers with proper expectations for the future.

Recognize that the customer has better things to do. They are working with you because they trust you to help them, but they are also eager to move on with their day.

By keeping closure at the forefront of every customer interaction, you not only enhance the overall experience but also build trust and loyalty. A customer who feels that their concerns were handled efficiently and effectively will be far more likely to return and recommend your service to others. Make every moment count and always work toward a successful resolution.

▶ **Adopt a solution-oriented mindset.**
As Stephen Covey advises in "The 7 Habits of Highly Effective People," always "begin with the end in mind" by focusing on the desired resolution from the start.

▶ **Set clear expectations.**
Let customers know what to expect and any next steps, so they always feel informed.

▶ **Stay committed to the resolution.**
Show that you genuinely care by following through and ensuring their issue is fully resolved.

▶ **Respect the customer's time.**
Be proactive, minimize delays, and keep them updated to avoid frustration.

▶ **Confirm satisfaction before ending the interaction.**
Ask, *"Is there anything else I can do for you today?"* to ensure they leave feeling valued and taken care of.

CHAPTER THIRTEEN
COMMANDMENT EIGHT

BE OPEN

"Your most unhappy customers are your greatest source of learning."

- **Bill Gates**

GIVE CREDENCE TO COMPLAINTS

Customer complaints aren't just inconveniences. They are invaluable insights. If you start seeing repeated issues, it's more than just an annoyance for the customer; it's a pattern that could be damaging your company's reputation. As a frontline representative, you are in a unique position to not only empathize with customers but also raise awareness of systemic problems.

If your company provides a way for customers to give direct feedback, let them know. Some of the most impactful policy and product improvements have come directly from customer complaints. Businesses that listen and adapt create better experiences and build lasting loyalty.

EVERYONE PLAYS A ROLE IN CUSTOMER SERVICE

"But I work behind the scenes. I never interact with customers. This doesn't impact me, right?"

Wrong.

At some point, everything your company does affects customer experience. Whether it's a software update that changes functionality, a manufacturing process that influences product quality, or a logistics decision that delays delivery, every department plays a role. If one part of the process is flawed, the whole customer experience can suffer. Complaints should never be shrugged off as "not my problem." They are a company-wide concern.

COMPLAINTS ARE A GIFT

In Japanese business culture, a customer complaint is viewed as a compliment. The reasoning is simple. Customers don't have to complain. They can just leave. If they took the time to tell you what went wrong, it means they believe your business is worth improving. Treat complaints as valuable feedback, not personal attacks.

A complaint handled well doesn't just resolve an issue. It can create a loyal customer. A problem ignored, however, *is* a lost customer. And lost customers don't just disappear quietly. They tell others.

HOW ONE RESTAURANT LOST A CUSTOMER FOR GOOD

A family of four visited a well-known steakhouse at a time when the restaurant was nearly empty. Despite this, their experience went from bad to worse.

It took 30 minutes to be seated and another 30 minutes just to place an order. When the silverware was unrolled, two dirty spoons were stuck together. A coupon, which was being accepted at other locations, was suddenly refused.

When they called later to speak to the manager, they were simply given a mailing address for corporate headquarters.

Frustrated, they wrote a letter detailing their experience. It was ignored. No response. No apology.

The next time they wanted steak, they chose a popular competitor, and they were treated well. That restaurant never got a second chance.

Ignoring complaints doesn't make them go away — it just ensures that customers do.

SURVEYS, STARS, AND THE THIRST FOR FEEDBACK.

I'll be honest: I've fallen into the survey trap too. In today's business world, stars aren't just feedback. They are currency. Google doesn't care how the customer felt. It cares how they *clicked*. I rely on that ecosystem to grow my business, so yes, I ask for reviews. But I do it in the quietest way I can: as the final line of a thank-you message, not the focus of the service. I believe, and have seen, that if quality comes first, the numbers take care of themselves. So far, they have.

Think about the difference between a big-box returns counter where customers wait 30 minutes to be told "you're in the wrong line," versus a place like Costco, where one worker stocks rotisserie chickens one day and gathers carts the next — and still remembers your name. One company obsesses over ratings and turnover. The other just builds trust slowly, consistently, and without asking for applause. They don't need to beg for five stars. Their stars walk back through the door every week.

▶ **Establish (or review) an escalation process.**
Ensure there's a clear pathway for handling complaints —
who gets involved, when issues should be escalated, and how
resolutions are tracked. If there's no formal process, propose
one.

▶ **Monitor and analyze complaints for patterns.**

▶ **Track recurring issues.**
Are multiple customers reporting the same problem (e.g.,
website glitches, product defects, billing errors)? If so,
escalate these concerns as systemic problems, not isolated
incidents.

▶ **Make sure someone is reviewing customer feedback.**
Whether it's poor reviews, survey responses, or direct emails,
designate a person or team to regularly assess and address
complaints instead of letting them pile up in an inbox.

▶ **Respond to all complaints — don't let them go
unanswered.**
Even if a full resolution isn't immediate, acknowledge the
issue, communicate next steps, and provide updates. Silence
signals indifference and drives customers away.

▶ **Close the loop with customers.**
If a complaint leads to a policy change, product fix, or service
improvement, let the customer know. This not only rebuilds
trust but also turns a dissatisfied customer into a loyal
advocate.

▶ **Train employees to view complaints as valuable.**
Shift the mindset from "dealing with complaints" to "learning
from customers." Encourage employees to welcome
feedback and suggest process improvements based on
common concerns.

CHAPTER FOURTEEN
COMMANDMENT NINE

BE WELCOMING

"Customers will never love a company until the employees love it first."

- **Simon Sinek**

CREATE AN INVITING WORKPLACE

Too often, workplaces are filled with "heads down, just-get-it-done" energy, where efficiency takes priority over engagement. Customers pick up on this. A lifeless environment, no matter how well-run, can feel cold and unwelcoming.

Contrast this with places where employees are engaged, enjoying their work, and making customers feel like part of the experience. One great example is the famous Seattle Fish Market, where employees enthusiastically call out orders, toss fish through the air, and interact with customers in a fun, energetic way. Their model goes beyond selling seafood. It creates an experience that draws people in and makes them want to be there. Native Seattleites and tourists alike flock there to buy their seafood, both for the product and the experience.

THE SHIFT TO SELF-SERVICE

The times are changing, and many businesses are moving toward the self-service model, automated checkouts, mobile ordering, and minimal human interaction. Even legendary retail giants like Sears and Montgomery Ward have shifted from large-format, big-box stores to a completely online model. While these approaches can be efficient, they lack warmth. If a customer never interacts with a real person, they may as well have just shopped online.

This makes it even more critical for businesses that *do* have in-person service to create an environment that feels alive. A friendly greeting, a quick joke, or an engaging atmosphere can set businesses apart in an era where genuine human interaction is becoming rare. You can even see this in companies with a strict online presence, like Amazon, offering a sense that they are inviting companies to work for.

THE BALANCE: FUN, BUT FOCUSED

Of course, there's a fine line. If employees are so caught up in their own fun that customers feel ignored, it backfires. Have you ever walked into a store where the staff were too busy chatting and laughing to acknowledge you? It's frustrating. The goal isn't just to have fun — it's to create an environment where *everyone*, customers included, feels welcome and valued.

A workplace that embraces fun fosters camaraderie, increases engagement, and can even improve productivity. Costume contests, fundraisers, team picnics, and casual get-togethers after work all contribute to a positive work culture. When employees genuinely enjoy where they work and the people they work with, that energy is often reflected in their interactions with customers. If that fun can be tied directly to the job — whether it's a friendly sales competition, themed dress-up days, or creative customer engagement events — even better. And if customers can be a part of it in a meaningful way, that's the best scenario.

The key to successfully integrating fun into the workplace is maintaining professionalism and being mindful of the customer's experience. Some activities are best kept behind the scenes. A casual Super Bowl pool or an employee's wedding announcement is great for morale, but it doesn't need to be broadcast to customers. If employees are joking loudly near customers, playing music that spills into public areas, or engaging in personal conversations while stocking shelves, it can quickly shift from creating a lively atmosphere to becoming an unprofessional distraction.

I've been to restaurants where the kitchen staff's banter was loud enough for customers to hear, making the entire experience feel chaotic rather than inviting. I've also been to stores where employees chatted about personal drama while stocking shelves, creating an uncomfortable atmosphere. On the other hand, I've seen workplaces where employees were relaxed, enjoying their work, and still keeping focus on the customers. There's a noticeable difference between an environment that is professionally casual and one that is just careless.

At the end of the day, fostering a fun, engaging workplace is essential. It should never come at the cost of customer experience. The best workplaces strike that perfect balance: employees are comfortable, customers feel welcome, and professionalism is never compromised. It becomes about the culture. Usually, that reflects the culture of the public's view of the business as well. It can be built over time but torn down in a matter of weeks.

THE ROLE OF TEAMWORK

A strong, inviting workplace isn't just about individual attitudes. It is about teamwork. Bob Farrell, founder of Farrell's Ice Cream Parlour, often pointed to migrating geese as the perfect teamwork example. When flying in a V formation, geese take turns at the front, leading the way and absorbing the brunt of the wind resistance. After a couple of minutes, the lead bird drifts back, and another moves up to take its place. This pattern continues seamlessly, with no egos, no confusion, just an efficient and shared workload that benefits the entire group.

For this kind of teamwork to work in a business setting, two key elements must be in place:

PROCESSES & FLEXIBILITY

Just like the geese instinctively rotate leadership, teams need clear processes and protocols to operate efficiently. In some industries, documenting these procedures is crucial. However, flexibility is just as important. Over-regulating can box a team in. A balance between structure and adaptability allows teams to perform at their peak.

When the McDonald brothers designed their first fast-food restaurant (McDonald's), they meticulously practiced each motion, perfecting the most efficient way to handle food prep, customer service, and cleanliness. They also knew the danger of monotony, so they rotated jobs every hour. This not only kept employees engaged but also ensured that everyone understood multiple roles, making the entire operation more dynamic and resilient.

SPEAKING UP & INNOVATING

Teamwork isn't just about following procedures. It should also be about improving them. If you see a way to enhance efficiency or create a better customer experience, speak up! Maybe you notice that Andrea is struggling with an outdated process, and you have a better idea. Sharing these insights helps your team, your business, and most importantly, your customer.

A dynamic, supportive workplace leads to better service, happier employees, and, ultimately, happier customers. When customers walk into an environment where people enjoy their work and collaborate effectively, they feel it — and they'll want to come back.

THE CONTACT CENTER THAT FORGOT PEOPLE

Back in 2014, I was between roles and interviewed for a Training Manager position at a local contact center. With 25 years in the industry, I knew what to expect (or at least I thought I did).

Instead of cubicles and a warm, organized environment, I walked into what looked like a warehouse. Metal desks sat in semi-circles, all facing *outward*. In the center of the room, about 8–10 feet off the ground, stood a crow's nest they called *AutoDesk*. From there, a few supervisors could monitor agent screens and live stats on massive reader boards along the back wall.

One board, labeled "Hustle Board," displayed a few kudos — by first initial and last name only. Most other boards simply showed call times, idle time, and who was "available." It felt cold, mechanical, and… watched. Break area? Just folding tables in the back. No real decorations. No warmth. No humanity.

During the interview, I asked the panel how long they had worked there and whether they'd been promoted from within. All of them had been there less than two years, and none had come from the call floor. That told me everything I needed to know.

I didn't get the job. And truthfully? I'm grateful. This wasn't a contact center. It was a command center. This was 2014, not 1914 (or 1984).

YOU CAN'T SERVE PEOPLE IN A COLD ROOM

Your environment, physical and emotional, is one of the few things you *can* control. And it matters more than you think.

You can't expect employees to deliver warmth, care, and humanity to customers if they feel watched, isolated, or replaceable. No amount of technology or tracking can replace a healthy, empowered culture.

As a leader, your space should reflect your values. Small gestures — like personal touches, spontaneous recognition, or even a shared snack in the breakroom — can shift everything. A positive environment doesn't happen by accident. It's a decision.

CASE STUDY:

WHAT LEADERSHIP REALLY LOOKS LIKE

Years before that warehouse interview, when I was first promoted to Training Manager, the Site Director pulled me aside and shared something I've never forgotten:

"Dan, I want to build a culture here," he told me. "We want people who want to be here — who feel like they're a part of something. We'll do the annual food drive, give back to the community, and maybe even block off a section of the parking lot one day and have a picnic "just because."

That culture? It starts in the classroom. Can you help make sure each new hire class feels the same warmth and investment the rest of the site does?"

That one conversation stuck with me almost two decades later.

In that earlier story, the warehouse-style call center, agents weren't even treated like customers. People operated under fear, not trust. There was no path forward, no connection, just observation and output.

In contrast, the team I eventually joined thrived. More than half the managers had been promoted from within. All of them had spent time on the front lines. That meant empathy wasn't something we had to teach. It was already there from a breadth of lived experience that shaped leadership. People didn't just show up for a paycheck; they showed up for each other.

And that's the difference.

It may not be possible to fix every policy or alter the workplace dynamic. However, individuals have the ability to change their contribution within it. You *can* speak up. You *can* make your corner of the room more human, more hopeful, more real, because when people feel seen and supported, they carry that forward to customers. And that's how culture spreads — one real interaction at a time.

▶ **Foster a Positive Atmosphere.**
Greet customers warmly, engage with them beyond just transactions, and create a welcoming environment where people feel valued.

▶ **Balance Fun with Focus.**
Prioritize customers while motivating employees to appreciate their work. Energy should enhance, not distract from, the customer experience.

▶ **Encourage Teamwork & Shared Responsibilities.**
Rotate roles when possible to keep tasks fresh and ensure everyone understands multiple aspects of the job, making the team more adaptable.

▶ **Allow for Process Improvements.**
Employees on the frontlines often see opportunities for improvement. Foster an environment that encourages feedback and suggestions.

▶ **Lead by Example.**
Management should model enthusiasm, engagement, and customer focus. A team takes cues from its leadership. If leaders create an inviting workplace, employees will follow.

CHAPTER FIFTEEN
COMMANDMENT TEN

BE MEMORABLE

"Always give people more than what they expect to get."

- **Nelson Boswell**

THE CHERRY ON TOP

This concept comes from the book "Give 'em the Pickle" by Bob Farrell, the founder of Farrell's Ice Cream Parlour. The story behind it is simple yet powerful. A regular customer loved the pickles at Farrell's and always asked for extra. The restaurant had always obliged, but one day, a server informed him there would be an extra charge. The customer, feeling unappreciated, left, never returned, and eventually wrote a letter explaining why. Bob Farrell heard the story years later and transformed it into a customer service philosophy that still resonates today.

The core lesson? Offer more than the customer expects. Provide that "extra something" that makes your business stand out from the rest.

Farrell's had been offering "pickles" long before this story gained traction:

Birthday celebrations were always a special spectacle for the guest of honor.

Certain menu items, like the "Portland Zoo" (A large group sundae that fed a dozen or more), triggered sirens and cheers, making it a memorable event for everyone in the restaurant.

Kids who came with their parents could select a small treat from the candy store when their bill was paid.

All of these little extras added up to an unforgettable experience that kept customers coming back. And when customers leave saying, "I'll be back!" (as Arnold Schwarzenegger made famous), you know you've done something right.

CHERRIES ON TOP IN BUSINESS

Every business has opportunities to give customers something more. That keeps them engaged, happy, and loyal.

Exceed expectations:

If you have the chance to wow a customer, take it. (For example, in the world of e-commerce, free shipping has become a simple yet powerful "cherry" that boosts sales.)

Surprise them with great service: Leave customers with a positive, lasting impression that makes them want to return.

Build a reputation:

Customers don't just talk about bad experiences — they love to share great ones too!

REAL WORLD CHERRIES

Many companies and individuals have created their own "cherries" that set them apart:

A garbage collector and his son:

"Every time we see someone struggling to start a lawnmower, we stop and help them. We can start any lawnmower!" This small act of kindness creates goodwill in the community.

Nordstrom:

Known for its legendary customer service, Nordstrom has a famously flexible return policy and even assigns personal shopping assistants to customers upon request.

Amazon:

Their introduction of free shipping on many orders skyrocketed customer satisfaction and loyalty. It became the tipping point that sent their sales into the stratosphere!

Loyalty cards:

Coffee shops, restaurants, and retailers keep customers coming back with punch cards and rewards programs that give them something extra for their continued business.

WHAT'S YOUR CHERRY ON TOP?

Think about your industry, your company, and your role. What can you do to go the extra mile for your customers? The best businesses recognize that it's the little things that make the biggest impact.

So, what's your cherry on top?

► **Identify Your "Cherries on Top."**
Find small, meaningful ways to add value to your customer's experience — whether it's a small freebie, an unexpected perk, or an extra touch of service.

► **Empower Employees to Go the Extra Mile.**
Encourage frontline staff to take initiative in making customers feel special, whether by offering small gestures of appreciation or solving problems proactively.

► **Make Exceptional Service a Habit.**
Build a company culture where exceeding expectations isn't just encouraged — it's the standard.

► **Personalize the Experience.**
Remember customer preferences, acknowledge repeat visitors, and make interactions feel unique and valued.

► **Look for Low-Cost, High-Impact Touches.**
Whether it's a handwritten thank-you note, free gift wrapping, or a simple warm greeting, small efforts create lasting impressions.

Giving customers more than they expect is what sets businesses apart. Whether it's a small perk, an act of kindness, or an unexpected level of service, these "cherries" create loyalty and lasting impressions. The best companies know that the little things aren't just extras — they're what make customers say, "I'll be back!

CHAPTER SIXTEEN

THE BOOK OF FIRE AND ICE

"If you can keep your head when all about you

Are losing theirs and blaming it on you..." from "IF — "

- **Rudyard Kipling**

DEALING WITH IRATE CUSTOMERS

Some customers are so jacked up and upset that nothing you say will please them. While we always aim to disarm an angry customer and de-escalate the situation, some cases go beyond what a single employee can handle. When a customer becomes threatening, profane, or completely out of control, it's critical to have a structured plan in place.

HAVE A CLEAR PROTOCOL

A company should have well-defined guidelines for handling irate customers, and every employee should be trained in these procedures before they ever hit the floor. If an employee has to decide in the moment what's allowed, what's not, and when to escalate, you're setting them up for failure. Make sure everyone knows the limits — how much abuse an employee is expected to take and at what point intervention happens.

Some companies have a "Three Strike" profanity rule, where the employee warns the customer after two instances, then is permitted to disengage on the third. Other businesses have a "Never Hang Up, Never Walk Away" policy, which might sound like great customer service, but at what cost? Are you forcing your frontline staff to become punching bags? Decide ahead of time what your company's stance is and communicate it clearly. If you are on the front lines, have that communication with your supervisor or HR team now, so you can react properly when that situation arises.

KNOW YOUR ESCALATION CHANNELS

When an irate customer refuses to de-escalate, who takes over? Knowing the next person in the chain of command can help avoid unnecessary conflict. Typically, we wait for the customer to request a supervisor, but if emotions are running too high, employees should feel empowered to initiate the escalation themselves. Never let your emotions become the problem.

In live settings, it's crucial to know who can step in — whether it's a security team, a supervisor, or another department. Communication tools, such as radios or escalation hotlines, should be readily available and well understood by the team.

THE VIP TREATMENT

For example, when I worked as an usher at Providence Park for the Portland Timbers, we had a strict protocol for handling belligerent or visibly intoxicated fans. If we identified a problem, we wouldn't act alone. Instead, we'd locate a teammate with a radio and request a supervisor using the code 'VIP' — Visibly Intoxicated Person. The closest supervisor would then come to my section, and I'd discreetly point out the person in question. If they agreed, security would be called in to help remove the individual from the general crowd. If the situation escalated further, the final step was to refund their ticket and escort them off the premises. But the key point here?

- We had a plan.
- We had clear steps.
- We didn't leave it up to individual judgment in the heat of the moment.

That's what every company needs.

Document the Incident

Once the situation has been handled, proper and swift documentation is key. If the customer returns later or the issue escalates further, the next employee needs to be aware of what has already transpired. No customer should have to explain their frustration twice. That only makes things worse. A well-documented case ensures that the company presents a consistent, informed response at every touchpoint.

Take a Breath Before Moving On

Dealing with an angry customer is mentally exhausting. Before taking your next call or greeting the next guest, take a moment to reset. The next person you speak to has no idea what just happened. They shouldn't feel any lingering frustration from the previous interaction. If necessary, talk to a supervisor or a teammate to decompress before diving back in.

The Profanity Rule

Let's be real, we know what we're talking about here. Some levels of frustration are understandable, but outright verbal abuse should not be tolerated. If a customer is venting about a product, service, or process, I can show some empathy. If it's directed at me personally, then we have new arrangements. Your company should have a policy on this, and it should be enforced consistently. If you're unsure how to handle it, escalate or debrief with a supervisor afterward. If there is no policy, offer to work with them to establish one. (For larger companies, be sure and get HR involved. [I know, I know]}

Stay in Control

It takes time to build confidence in handling these interactions. But remember — if you remain calm when the world around you is losing its head, you stay in control. Your goal is not to win an argument; it's to channel the customer's frustration into a resolution. Focus on the problem, not the person, and you'll walk away from even the toughest interactions with your professionalism — and sanity — intact.

PUTTING IT TO PRACTICE:

▶ **Review and Understand Your Company's Policy.**
Take time to review your company's guidelines for handling difficult customers. If they don't exist or are unclear, ask a supervisor for clarification. Be *very clear* on your company's policy on handling profanity. (If no process or policy exists, perhaps offer to work with them to establish one!)

▶ **Practice De-escalation Techniques.**
Use active listening and empathy to diffuse tense situations. Avoid reacting emotionally. Take a deep breath before responding.

▶ **Know Your Escalation Plan.**
Identify who to call when a situation gets out of control. Familiarize yourself with tools like escalation hotlines, security contacts, or supervisor handoffs.

▶ **Document Every Major Incident.**
If a customer interaction goes south, record key details for future reference. Ensure your notes are clear, concise, and accessible to colleagues who may handle the issue later.

▶ **Take a Mental Reset.**
After handling a tough customer, step away for a moment to clear your mind. Talk to a teammate or supervisor if needed. Do not carry frustration into the next interaction.

CHAPTER SEVENTEEN

THE BOOK OF APPROACH

"Just because you are doing more, doesn't mean you are getting more done."

- **Denzel Washington**

THE THREE STEPS TO A SUCCESSFUL INTERACTION

From the Author:

Because you are, in effect, my customer, I want to offer you something extra — my personal "cherry" for you!

These steps will help you in any situation, whether you're troubleshooting a problem, making a sale, or simply working through a customer request. This simple formula ensures you are thinking clearly, handling discussions effectively, and setting yourself up for success.

Ask Open-Ended Questions

Allow the customer to guide the conversation until you fully understand their needs and expectations.

Paraphrase and Gain Agreement

Confirm your understanding with the customer before moving forward.

Ask Closed-Ended Questions

Shift control back to you, leading to a quick resolution.

STEP 1: ASK OPEN-ENDED QUESTIONS

Open-ended questions give you valuable details. The more information you have, the better you can help. These questions do not have simple yes/no answers and instead encourage customers to share their full story.

Each answer should guide you toward the next question, just like a funnel narrowing toward the final answer. Listening well builds customer confidence in you.

Example questions:

- What are you looking to accomplish today?
- Can you walk me through what's happening?
- What challenges have you run into?

STEP 2: PARAPHRASE AND GAIN AGREEMENT

This step reassures the customer that:

- You were actively listening and fully understanding their request.
- You have a clear idea of how to help.
- You're prepared to offer a credible solution.

Paraphrasing can be as simple as repeating back an order, summarizing a request, or confirming key details:

"So, what you're saying is, you need [X] to work like [Y]. Does that sound right?"

Once the customer confirms your understanding, you're in the best position to move forward with a solution.

Important Note for Sales Representatives:

The transition from paraphrasing to a closed-ended question is the perfect time to *ask for the business.*

Asking for the Business is the most often missed step in closing a sales opportunity. If you put the question in the right place in the conversation, it can be very easy. Once you've clarified the issue and the customer agrees with your solution, use this opportunity **to** move the sale forward:

- "Would you like me to book that for you?"
- "Should I set up that appointment?"
- "Can I go ahead and write up that order?"

This creates a natural bridge to the third and final step — dotting the i's and crossing the t's — where you confirm details and ensure a smooth completion of the interaction.

STEP 3: ASK CLOSED-ENDED QUESTIONS

Now that you and the customer are aligned, shift to yes/no questions to finalize the interaction. These questions keep the process moving efficiently.

Examples:

Does this solution work for you?

- "Would you like to proceed with this option?"
- "Is there anything else I can assist with today?"
- A final confirmation — "Did this meet your expectations?" — ensures that the customer is satisfied prior to their departure.

How This Works in Real Life

You already see this process in action every day:

Ordering Food at a Restaurant

Open-ended: "What would you like today?"
Paraphrase: "So that's a burger, no onions, with a side of fries?"
Closed-ended: "Would you like anything else?"
Final confirmation: "How is everything? Can I get you a refill?"

Home Improvement Store

"What kind of project are you working on?"
"So, you're installing a new light fixture and need the right wiring supplies?"
"Would these materials work for you?"

Buying a Used Car

"What will you be using the car for?"
"So you're looking for a reliable SUV under $20,000?"
"If I find one that matches, would you like to take it for a test drive?"

CASE STUDY: ROB IS THE MAN

One of the best examples of this method in action is a well-known used car salesman. He's a real guy, I'll call him Rob. He was so exceptional at selling cars that dealerships across the country hired him to clear their inventory efficiently. Many young salespeople shadowed him, trying to replicate his success, but his results were unmatched.

Here's how Rob worked his magic:

Step 1: Open-Ended Questions

Build Rapport and Gather Information

When a potential customer entered the lot, Rob wouldn't immediately start showcasing cars. Instead, he'd invite the guests into the waiting area — a comfortable, low-pressure environment. He then pulled out a small legal pad and began asking open-ended questions. Keep in mind, he knows the entire lot's inventory by heart. He took the time to learn about each vehicle on the lot and insisted on being informed when another salesperson sells a car, so he would not consider it.

- Why are you in the market for a new vehicle?
- What will you use the car for?
- Who will be the primary driver?
- What features are most important to you?
- What year range are you considering?
- What is your budget?
- Do you have a favorite brand?

What colors do you prefer?

Look at that funnel again. With each question, the funnel narrows until he's narrowed the options to just two models that best matched the customer's needs.

Step 2: Paraphrase and Gain Agreement

Once he identified the top two models, he took the customer directly to those cars. More often than not, the customer would be amazed at how well they matched their needs, saving them the frustration of browsing the entire lot.

Rob would then offer test drives on both models. By the time the test drives were complete, he'd ask a straightforward question:

"If we can make the numbers work, do you want to drive this home today?"

Step 3: Closed-Ended Questions

Closing the Sale

This question subtly transitions the customer from browsing mode to buying mode. If they responded with, "Yeah, I think so," or "Let's take a look at the numbers," Rob knew the deal was nearly closed. From there, he took charge of finalizing the sale.

Breaking Down Rob's Winning Strategy

Rob's approach is a textbook example of this as a sales framework:

Open-Ended Questions

He starts by gathering crucial information in a non-pushy way (Who will drive? What features matter most?).

Paraphrasing and Gaining Agreement

He presents the best options and asks, "If we can make this work, is this the kind of car you're looking for?" This step subtly asks for the sale.

Closed-Ended Questions

He finalizes the deal by transitioning into a direct but comfortable close: "Let's complete the sale and get you on your way."

WHY THIS WORKS EVERYWHERE

Rob's method isn't just for car sales or even sales. It works for job interviews, meetings, and casual conversations — it's applicable across all industries. Large corporations and small businesses alike implement a similar framework because it works. This isn't new information. It is just a structured approach to what great salespeople and front-line customer service people intuitively do. By following this framework, any customer service professional can enhance their sales skills and improve conversion rates while keeping the customer's experience smooth and enjoyable.

CASE STUDY: THE AUTHOR'S INTAKE CALLS

I apply this process in my current Notary Public business. As a Mobile Notary Public, I primarily work out of my car, providing notary services to clients who need me to come to them to sign and notarize their documents. To establish confidence and begin building rapport, I follow this same structured process during each initial customer interaction. Here's an example of how it unfolds:

Scenario:

Notarizing a Power of Attorney document in a senior living facility

For this example, Mr. Smith is calling to arrange for a notary to visit his mother's residence at a senior living facility to sign a Power of Attorney document.

Caller:

"Hello, I'm looking for a notary to help my mother sign a Power of Attorney document. She lives in a senior residence facility in the suburbs."

Open-Ended Questions

Me: "That's great. I'd be happy to assist. Where is she currently living?"
Caller: "She's at Great Western Village on Main Street."
Me: "Oh, I know that place well! I visit there frequently. Do you already have the documents?"
Caller: "Yes, we do."
Me: "May I ask how they were prepared?"
Caller: "Her lawyer prepared them."

Me: "That's good. Are there any additional documents you may need, such as an Advance Directive or a Last Will?"

Caller: "No, we've already taken care of those. We just need this one notarized."

Me: "If this is as you mentioned, then the cost for this appointment should be around $60. Is that okay with you?

Caller: "Yes, that sounds about right."

Paraphrase and Gain Agreement

Me: "Perfect. I will be at Great Western Village on Monday afternoon at 2:00 p.m. to notarize the Power of Attorney document with Carla Smith in Room #203. We've discussed the cost. Does that sound okay?"

Caller: "Yes, that sounds great."

Closed-Ended Questions

Me: "Excellent. Before we proceed, I have a few more important questions:

- Does she have her identification with her?
- Is she able to sign her name?
- Can she hold a conversation?
- Does she speak English?
- Most importantly, is this something she wants to do?

Caller: "Yes, everything is in order."

Me: "Great! I look forward to meeting you both on Monday."

Why This Approach Works

- Establishes rapport
- Mentioning familiarity with the location reassures the client
- Ensures document readiness
- Confirming preparation prevents delays
- Clarifies additional needs
- Asking about related documents ensures completeness
- Verifies the signer's capability
- Ensures compliance with legal requirements

This structured intake process allows me to provide professional, efficient, and legally compliant notary services while making the client feel at ease.

Step 3A – Check Your Work

This step isn't always possible, depending on the nature of your business, but if you can, follow up with your customer to see if the solution you provided was truly helpful.

In my notary business, I don't typically call clients for feedback, but I always send a follow-up thank-you note as a professional courtesy. A small gesture like this reinforces goodwill and leaves a lasting impression.

Of course, in some industries, follow-ups don't make sense. You wouldn't call back a fast-food customer or a grocery shopper to check on their experience. However, in businesses where relationships matter, a simple follow-up can set you apart.

▶ **Are you asking the right questions at the right time?**
Most service failures aren't about attitude — they're about timing and technique. Review your typical interactions and identify where you tend to jump too quickly to a solution. Could more open-ended questions up front help you get it right the first time?

▶ **Have you created your own conversation script?**
Every business has unique language, jargon, and situations. Create a sample script or flow that fits your specific customer journey — one that walks through an open-ended start, a paraphrased checkpoint, and a confident close. Practicing this will help you sound natural and prepared.

▶ **Does your work allow for a clear finish or follow-up?**
Some jobs end with a handshake; others end with a tracking number or formal sign-off. Identify how you know when a task is "done" — and whether you could build in a brief confirmation or follow-up step to make sure the customer agrees that it's complete and they are satisfied.

▶ **Can you use this process outside of work?**
Try this method in a volunteer setting, during a project meeting, or even when helping a friend solve a problem. Once you get comfortable with the rhythm — explore, confirm, close — you'll find it applies far beyond your day job.

THE POWER OF THREE

"Clear Eyes. Full Hearts. Can't Lose"

– **Coach Eric Taylor** (Friday Night Lights)

SOME FINAL THOUGHTS

Early in his career, actor Tom Hanks was rehearsing a Shakespeare play in the theater. The rehearsal wasn't going well. The director was off, each performer was struggling, and the entire scene felt chaotic and disconnected. Finally, the director couldn't take it anymore. He stood up and shouted, "Stop! Everybody stop!"

Then, he offered a piece of advice that stuck with Hanks for the rest of his career.

"I can do some of this for you," the director said. "Shakespeare did some of it for you, too. But for this to work, *you've* got to be in the moment as well. I'm really only asking three things from you. Your talent will carry you the rest of the way. But I need three things:

- Be on time. (Which really means be a little early.)

- Know the text. (In acting, that means knowing your lines —
  and the lines around yours that matter. In everything else, it
  simply means know what you're doing.)
- Have a head full of ideas. Come prepared. Bring something
  to the table that will make this better. Have a plan."

As a young actor, Hanks had to sit with that for a moment. But it made
sense. And looking back, he considers it the best advice he ever
received.

Interestingly, the same idea echoed from another corner of excellence.
Legendary football coach and broadcaster John Madden had a similar
rule of three for his players. They were his only "Team Rules:"

- Be on time.
- Stop and listen.
- Work your butt off.

That's it. Simple. Powerful. Effective.

So while I may have given you a whole list of customer service
"commandments" throughout this book, Tom Hanks and Coach
Madden remind us that sometimes, all it takes is three.

And these aren't just rules from celebrity figures. They come from
people universally recognized for being humble, talented, and
consistently excellent at what they do. No scandals, no fluff, just pure
mastery of their craft.

Which brings us full circle.

Whether you're acting on a stage, coaching a team, or running a
business — especially one built around serving customers — these
three principles still apply:

1. Be on time.
2. Know what you're doing.
3. Bring your best ideas.

I've broken down how this looks through the eye of customer service
throughout this book. My hope is that you've seen how

interconnected it all is. If you can adopt even just a few of these principles, you'll be *your best business*. I have no doubts about your success. Your customers will notice. They'll thank you. And they'll be back.

Enjoy the journey

.

EPILOGUE

STAND TALL IN THE STORM

April 2025

Over the past 25 years, we've weathered more than a few economic and social storms. From 9/11 to Hurricane Katrina, the large and devastating fires that took over the west coast and other parts of the country as well as other devastating natural disasters, to the 2008 housing crash, and of course, the unforgettable chaos of 2020 — COVID, civil unrest, more fires, hurricanes, typhoons, tornados, and the collective exhaustion that came with all of it. And now, here in 2025, we once again find ourselves standing at the edge of economic uncertainty, with talk of a looming recession and unstoppable inflation creeping in.

Times like these put the world on edge. Consumers become more cautious, scaling back their spending and redefining what "essential" really means. And in these moments, something else also happens. Customer care often takes a hit. We all saw it during COVID. Attitudes soured, patience wore thin, and service slipped. At a time when people needed empathy the most, it was sometimes in its shortest supply.

But here's what I believe: this is your moment!

When your competitors are stumbling, and let's face it, you might be too, this is not the time to retreat. It is the time to rise. Your customers need you now more than ever, not just for what you offer, but for how you make them feel in the midst of uncertainty.

I won't point fingers or pretend to have all the answers about inflation, policy, or global markets. But I *will* ask you to do one thing. Stand firm and lead with gratitude. Even when it's hard. Especially when it's hard.

If you commit to your customers during the storm — if you continue to care, to listen, and to serve with authenticity — they'll remember. And when the skies clear, they won't just come back. They'll become your fiercest, most loyal advocates.

Don't let the times drag you down. You have more influence than you realize.

Let your attitude be the anchor. I promise — it will carry you further than you think!

ACKNOWLEDGEMENTS

"If I have seen further, it is by standing on the shoulders of Giants."

– Sir Isaac Newton

I WOULD LIKE TO THANK THE ACADEMY...

Each year, I hear someone give a lengthy thank-you speech, nervously trying to avoid leaving anyone out. Now I know how they feel. So let me start here: thank you to everyone I've ever met since birth. (Okay — most of you.) Whether you know it or not, you shaped this book in some way. But I'm not blessed with unlimited pages, so for now, please know this: your influence is here, even if your name isn't.

This book began as a training assignment/project and turned into a labor of love. I owe that turn to Carl Moyer and Van Green, who assigned me this work 25 years ago and believed that customer service truly mattered. David Baker followed through to assure the excellence was maintained.

I learned early lessons from my first jobs, especially from my mom and her team at Ace Pet, and from the managers and friends at Pietro's Pizza Parlour, a few of whom are still there four decades later. I can still make any pizza on the menu.

In the contact center world, too many great colleagues to name helped shape this content, but I must mention Pam M., my first manager and longtime friend. Carl Moyer appears again here, along with my Yahoo! teammates, many of whom shaped both my work and my thinking.

At Stream SGS, I was a part of the best training team around. Thanks for being the early test audience and pushing this content forward. You continued to advocate for customer excellence and never deterred. Chuck R., David K., and Brian P. deserve a special mention. David also assisted with the proofreading of this volume. Dan Roos was also a continuous friend and confidante during that important time.

Throughout this book, I've been careful to avoid naming individuals directly, changing names where needed so no one feels singled out unfairly. But in a few special cases, Valeria, Trae and Sarah, Gerron, Corwin, Audrey at McDonald's, Emily at Subway, Marcy, Luanna, and Leslie, you were the bright spots that gave me hope throughout this journey. I also need a special shout-out to Becky at Postal Works and her team (Debi, Tracy, Claudia and Dan.) If you thought I was talking about you... I was. Thank you for setting such a powerful example.

As for the others, the 'yang' to your 'yin', they'll remain anonymous, which is better than they did for us.

As a notary, I've leaned heavily on the wisdom of Laura Biewer and Bill Soroka. Bill was the one who said, "You know, this could be a book." And here we are.

Joe Dudman has been a dear friend, reality check and cheerleader for 35 years. His wife, Charissa Yang, was a generous proofreader and supporter throughout. Neither of them said no whenever I called to ask their opinion or help on, well...anything. Thank you both.

Thanks to John Doherty and the team at EditorNinja for the precision editing of this copy.

To my parents, Bob and Mary Brewer — thank you for setting the foundation. My dad taught and played music. My mom modeled customer care and demanded the same. My sister Barbara and her family have been there every step of the way. We were a tight-knit family that learned as a key value to live by the Golden Rule – a theme present throughout this book. I was very lucky.

I'm proud of my roots in Milwaukie, Oregon, and the many people and communities that shaped me — especially the Oregon Road Runners Club and the running community, the North Clackamas Baseball and Softball Associations, and the many players I had the privilege to coach, and the Oaks Skating Club. I'm also grateful to the classrooms and colleagues I had the pleasure of working with at Whitford Middle and Aloha High, and to my Toastmasters friends — especially Eric Winger, Lorri Andersen, and Valerie Preston — whose encouragement helped shape this book.

I cannot leave out the Mustangs. My High School class and the Milwaukie High alumni before and after. We are a tight knit clan and I cannot believe we are still best friends all these almost 50 years later. "Onward, Victorious!"

I'd feel very bad if I did not mention the many friends and basketball officials, partners and and administrators I got to work with over 30 years (and over 4,000 games) in the Portland Basketball Officials Association. If there was ever a testing ground for customer service, it was there. I thank everyone from the Commissioner on down.

At Portland State University, I was fortunate to learn from inspiring mentors like Dr. Jim Heath and Dr. Ben Padrow, whose influence remains with me, and to share both community and conversation with Dr. Alan Cabelly, a friend from the running world whose example continues to guide me. My professors and colleagues at Portland State helped sharpen my voice and strengthen my values during pivotal years of my life.

Finally, to my wife Mary and my son Ian: every day with you teaches me something new about life, service, and love. You're my heart. I cannot say thank you enough.

As Hillary Clinton wrote, "It takes a village." Mine has been incredible. And as Matthew McConaughey said, "Gratitude reciprocates." I'm grateful to you all — and I hope you'll pay it forward.

SUGGESTED READING

The following books were instrumental in designing this curriculum:

"Give 'Em the Pickle!" – Robert Farrell (Available on Amazon)

"Fish!: A Remarkable Way to Boost Morale and Improve Results" – Stephen Lundin, Harry Paul, and John Christensen

"The Seven Habits of Highly Effective People" – Stephen R. Covey

"The Winner Within" – Pat Riley

"Customers for Life" – Carl Sewell

"The Nordstrom Way" – Robert Spector

"Built from Scratch: How a Couple of Regular Guys Grew The Home Depot from Nothing to $30 Billion" – Bernie Marcus & Arthur Blank

"The Toyota Way: 14 Management Principles from the World's Greatest Manufacturer" – Jeffrey K. Liker

ABOUT THE AUTHOR

"Do not do once, what you are not prepared to do a-thousand times!" –

Daniel Brewer

Daniel Brewer is a corporate trainer, mobile notary, caregiver, and lifelong volunteer based in Portland, Oregon. His customer service career began in 1974 — slinging pizza and soaking up early lessons in hospitality — and he has since trained thousands of professionals across a wide range of industries.

Over the past 50 years, Dan has worked across service sectors including retail, food service, contact centers, technical support, media distribution, hospitality, nonprofit leadership, and notary work. He has delivered training for major organizations including Disney, Yahoo!, Comcast, Dell, Microsoft, Adobe, AT&T, Coldwell Banker Realty, and Greater Giving. His focus has always been on practical service, clear communication, and doing right by the customer — even when the script runs out.

Known as a no-nonsense customer advocate who balances warmth with real-world insight, Daniel's workshops and talks blend humor, history, and hands-on tactics that help teams serve their customers and clients better without losing their humanity.

Outside of training, Daniel runs a successful mobile notary business and volunteers extensively with community organizations ranging from Toastmasters to the Oregon Road Runners Club and the Portland Basketball Officials Association. He lives in Portland with his wife and son and continues to speak, write, and coach others on building customer service that lasts.

Connect with Daniel Brewer on LinkedIn:
linkedin.com/in/dsbrewer

info@custservguru.com

"Daniel's book is a clear, practical guide to creating memorable service experiences. His stories illustrate timeless principles with warmth and wisdom. This is a resource I'll keep close — it speaks not only to notaries, but to anyone who serves customers and wants to stand out for the right reasons." — **Laura B., National Notary Trainer**

"The lessons in this book are simple but powerful. Daniel captures what many organizations forget: customers remember how you made them feel. His Ten Commandments of Customer Service are actionable and easy to implement, making this an essential tool for managers, teams, and anyone striving to deliver excellence daily." — **Chuck R., Technical Writer and Trainer**

"Daniel distills decades of experience into insights that are fresh and accessible. What I appreciate most is how practical his guidance is — you can read a chapter in the morning and apply it the same day. This book is an engaging roadmap for building trust and keeping customers coming back." — **Namitha S., Engineer**

"Dan Brewer has written a remarkable guide to winning with customer service. Packed with real examples and practical recommendations, it's accessible and actionable. Whether you lead one person or a thousand, this book belongs in every hand — a roadmap to building a team customers truly love." — **Chris T., Technical Team Leader**

"My organization usually frowns on customer experience training, but this book has a real shot. Dan's approach is practical, accessible, and surprisingly motivating. If his principles can resonate here, they can work anywhere. A refreshing take on service that could even move the needle inside the DMV." — **Patricia M., Department of Motor Vehicles**

THE TEN COMMANDMENTS OF CUSTOMER SERVICE

Commandment One: Be Nice. Be Kind. Be Respectful.
- Treat others as you would want to be treated.

Commandment Two: Be Awesome
- Strive to always be learning and be great at your job.

Commandment Three: Be Present
- Be there for your customers.

Commandment Four: Be Positive
- Set the tone for the customer's interaction.

Commandment Five: Be Sincere
- Lend an ear. Be willing to offer a genuine solution.

Commandment Six: Be Clear
- Communicate well.

Commandment Seven: Be Resolute.
- Work towards closure. "Begin with the end in mind."

Commandment Eight: Be Open.
- Give credence to complaints.

Commandment Nine: Be Welcoming.
- Create an inviting work environment.

Commandment Ten: Be Memorable.
- The "Cherry on Top"

THREE STEPS FOR A SUCCESSFUL INTERACTION

Step One: Ask open-ended questions.

Step Two: Paraphrase and gain agreement.

Step Three: Ask closed-ended questions.

    Step 3a: Confirm resolution (if possible).

www.ingramcontent.com/pod-product-compliance
Lightning Source LLC
Chambersburg PA
CBHW071416210326
41597CB00020B/3528